# Choosing Gladness

## LETTING GOD OCCUPY YOUR HEART

*(Study guide included)*

Julie Anderson

**HillCrest**
PUBLISHING

**HillCrest**
PUBLISHING

1648 Campus Court
Abilene, TX 79601
www.hillcrestpublishing.com

**Type Specifications:** Headline set in Apple Chancery, Bold, 36 point, 90% width. Subhead set in Apple Chancery, Italics, 18 point. Body copy set in Book Antiqua, 12 point. Endnote set in Book Antiqua, 10 point.

Printed in the United States of America

ISBN 0-89112-441-1
Library of Congress Card Number 00-103923

2,3,4,5

# Contents

# Introduction: The Power of Influence

My two-year-old mimics me. When he pointedly copies my words or actions, I usually cannot suppress my laughter. Like when I told him to "Go to sleep" and he turned to my sister lying next to him, shook a little finger at her and said, "Go sweep, go sweep!" Or when he picked up the remote phone, cradled it on his shoulder, and walked around the house gibbering in toddler-tongue, but gesturing his hands and raising his eyebrows Mommy-style. I laughed, and moaned, at this one recently: Luke watched me enjoy a swallow from my morning jug of chocolate milk and place the jug on the counter. He reached for the milk, so I gave him the jug. He dramatically savored a giant swig (like Mommy), smacked his lips, and then returned the milk to the counter. Only he couldn't quite reach the counter. The jug tipped backward and a fountain of chocolate milk cascaded through his blonde hair, ran rivers down the back of his neck, and dribbled into his diaper. After one of these copy-cat occasions, I usually telephone my mom or a friend and relish the moment.

I remember another occasion a few months ago when Luke was quick to mimic my actions.

However, the last thing I wanted to do was call and share the experience with anyone. In fact, I looked around to make sure my husband was not watching. I had just finished one of my "moments," as I call them. For six years of marriage I've challenged my husband with this uncanny trait of remembering every trial, each unfair situation, and any bit of earthly turmoil we've encountered. I can rattle them off on a whim, like a grocery list.

On this particular day, I had launched my moment by reacting despondently to our latest unpleasantry. (Right now I honestly cannot remember the specific occurrence or chain of events which spurred my attitude of despair.) As usual, I then proceeded to remind Lane of various misfortunes throughout our marriage. You know what I'm talking about: career struggles, health problems, relationship challenges, high interest rates, a "new" used car that breaks down immediately. I was building a snowball. I rolled this most recent bout of circumstantial unhappiness with all of the other difficult moments in our lives and, BAM!, I plopped this giant ball on our living room carpet, shaking the floor and rattling the walls. Then, I closed out my moment with tears. It was here that Luke jumped in. He curled his little fingers into his palms, crinkled up his tiny nose, covered his eyes, and made a moaning sound. He even rocked his little diaper-clad body to and fro, ever so slightly. Just like Mommy.

At that second, I knew my moments needed to stop.

After my moments come my guilt, my realization of our countless blessings, and my sincere and tearful apologies and appeals for forgiveness. Lane, a heaven-bound man with a spiritual maturity

I aspire to develop, graciously accepts my apologies and reminds me of his own weaknesses.

But how do I explain my moments to my two-year-old? How will I explain them to any future children I may have? Of course, later in life I will be able to discuss my imperfections with my children and apologize when necessary. And while small children may not always comprehend what is going on around them, I do believe they absorb more than we realize. Obviously, Luke absorbed my actions to the point at which he was able to mimic them.

These moments have taught me how quickly one person can tarnish the disposition of another. For instance, Lane will come home from work with a smile on his face, a spring in his step, and a hug just waiting to be enjoyed. But I can launch a moment, and by the end of my discourse of dissatisfaction, the spring in Lane's step is suddenly gone.

This is not a self-degradation book. I do not believe myself to be a poor wife or mother. Rather, I am a 28-year-old Christian woman who has come to a poignant realization: My attitude and behavior can influence, and in the case of children actually shape, the attitude and actions of those around me.

My moments allowed me to witness the contagious nature of negative thoughts and expressions. It seemed my unpleasantness actually cast a gray cloud over the room.

But what about the contagious nature of a positive attitude? Indeed, our home is not one of drudgery, and I've seen how laughter can spread throughout a room. I've seen how the good mood of one can take the sting off the bad mood of another. I've tickled the grouchiness out of my son and hugged the frustration out of my husband.

I have now come to grips with my power of influence (a power everyone possesses). In the case of my children, it's not only power, but responsibility.

These realizations have led me to look inwardly and study my influence on those around me, particularly my family.

I am not overwhelmed with self-disappointment, but I admit to a lack of consistency. When things are going well, I'm great. I laugh, tickle, hug, smile, and spread gladness. But when small or large unpleasantries come my way, I am easily shaken and am quick to display my unrest, agitation, or even despair. This makes for a bumpy home life, filled with up-and-down moments that can be and have been challenging.

I want to smooth out these bumps and strive to exert a consistently positive influence on my family. This calls for a consistently positive attitude that will shape me and my reactions to circumstances, rather than allowing circumstances to shape my attitude and behavior.

Of course, I realize I will encounter trials, large and small, that for a time take pleasure out of earthly living. However, as I reflect on the challenges I have already met, I realize I need to cultivate an attitude that will temper my disappointment or sadness with perseverance, faith, and an understanding that I can give God control of my sorrow.

I want my children to remember a Mom who enjoyed life. I would like them to remember a Mom who strived to make each day a pleasant one, who shared her gladness and gratitude in times of joy and her endurance and hope (not despair) in times of trial.

In twenty years, I want my children to look back on their home and say, "It was good to be there." I now realize I cannot do this alone. Thankfully, God does not expect me to.

# 1
# Gladness, Step-by-Step

*"This is the day the Lord has made; let us rejoice and be glad in it"*
—Psalms 118:24

*Glad*, adj. Experiencing or exhibiting joy and pleasure; *providing* joy and pleasure; pleased; willing; *of cheerful disposition* (American Heritage Dictionary, emphases mine).

Ideally, I should wake up each morning with the full, clear knowledge that the sunlight filtering through my mini-blinds means God has chosen to make a new day. The mere facts that an awesome and loving God chose to create this gift of a new day, and that I am a recipient of this gift should be enough to fashion within me a desire to rejoice and give me an attitude of gladness. Simply put, God made the day; I will be glad in the day God made.

But, from the moment I draw my first deep breath, complications, many beyond my control, begin to arise...

- God made the day...but I woke up with a splitting headache.
- God made the day...but the baby is irritable.

- God made the day...but my company is downsizing, and I'm scared to go to work.
- God made the day...but the house payment has to be mailed this morning, and it's already late.
- God made the day...but Sue hurt my feelings and I need time to get over it.
- God made the day...but I have too much to do, and there's no way I can get it all done.

Perhaps some struggle with truly painful challenges...

- God made the day...but the cancer is still here.
- God made the day...but my child is tragically ill.

The list could go on and on.

I want to be glad—to provide pleasure for myself, my friends, and family, while emanating a cheerful disposition. I want others to enjoy my presence, rather than breathe a collective sigh of relief when I exit the room. I've finally lived long enough to realize that my mood and my attitude can and will affect my family, my friends, my co-workers, my fellow Christians, and my neighbors. I can build people up, or I can drag them down. I can influence the morale of my entire office or family for better or worse.

When my son started mimicking my unpleasant moments, I reached a personal crossroads. I had no choice but to discover how to be glad—not just the concept, but the method.

I'm a little embarrassed to think that I found a verse I liked in the Bible, shut my Bible, and turned to my big blue dictionary to look for the rest of the answer. I liked the *American Heritage Dictionary* definition of "glad," and I believed it applied to Psalm 118:24. In my quest to improve rather than impoverish my surroundings, I wanted to exhibit joy and cheerfulness. But I needed more. God was telling me to rejoice and be glad. Perhaps he would tell me how. Perhaps, in the rest of his word, I would learn more about why.

When I began my quest for gladness, a friend and I were studying various books of the Bible together. Have you ever read a favorite book, chapter or verse over and over, only to find that one day the passage leaps off of the page and speaks to you like never before? You actually feel a tingle, a spark of joy, because God has spoken to you so personally, so directly. As I read the following verse, I did a mental double take. I knew I had tapped into the answer:

> "He seldom reflects on the days of his life, because God keeps him occupied with gladness of heart" (Ecclesiastes 5:20).

Ecclesiastes is Solomon's reflection on the days of his life and the various paths he took in his search for meaning and happiness. He tried wisdom, pleasures, and folly and found dead ends. He encountered the injustices and inequities that befall every man, and he witnessed the oppression of others. He warns us that life will be valleys and peaks, and we must accept the unchangeable.

Throughout the book, including Chapter 5, Solomon interjects his solution for meaning and satisfaction: True joy and fulfillment are found in God. Solomon builds on this principle with wonderful verses such as 3:12-13:

> I know that there is nothing better for men than to be happy and do good while they live.

> That everyone may eat and drink, and find
> satisfaction in all his toil—this is the gift of
> God.

What a bonus! We can find satisfaction while toiling!

Ecclesiastes 5:20 is another key element of Solomon's counsel on living joyful lives. I believe this verses begins to teach us, in step-by-step fashion, how to grow gladness.

Keep in mind, the Bible is wonderfully blended together. Psalm 118:24 inspired my desire for gladness. Ecclesiastes 5:20 kindled my exploration of the method of gladness. Countless other verses are woven into the tapestry of gladness of heart, mind, soul, and attitude. God didn't just say, "Be glad." Through the Bible, he gave us the who, what, when, where, why, and how of gladness. Not dictionary gladness. Not worldly gladness, but godly gladness.

Mix the words "God" and "glad," and the term "gladness" takes on richer meaning. This type of gladness is not a giddy sort of emotion characterized by a pep-rally mentality. Rather, this is gladness with depth, anchored in the knowledge of a God, possession of a Spirit, and security of the saved. When grown properly, godly gladness is rooted in such deep, rich soil that it blooms in every facet of our lives: thoughts, words, tone, attitude, actions, facial expressions, body language, decision-making—everything is transformed by the beauty of the gladness bloom.

That's the type of gladness I wanted to grow.

Almost two years later, I can testify to the fruits of the gladness of God. I look back on my despairing outbursts not with overwhelming shame, but with thankfulness that God has shown me a better way. I've realized that growing gladness is a continual process, one I will need to work on each new day. Satan loves to lead me into one of my old moments, but I have at my disposal the strength of a God who gave me a spiritual armor.

Now that I've tapped into the gladness of God, every day has the potential for brightness and sweetness. Perhaps in the midst of sorrow or struggle, the only bright spot will be the reality of heaven — but still the bright spot is there. If a day is seemingly void of gladness, it's not because God left me empty. Rather, I chose to ignore God's gladness in that day.

Some of the fruits of godly gladness may appeal to you: peace of mind, tranquil relationships, strength through storms, or spiritual depth. When you become a person of gladness, you will change not only your life, but the lives of those around you. Whether they realize it or not, people will respond to the gladness in you. Some may even ask you what has happened. And you can tell them God.

# Study Guide

1. Reflect on yesterday. If a neutral onlooker were to categorize your attitude, would he label your disposition as:
   a) glad
   b) unpleasant
   c) up and down

2. When you wake up in the morning, do you look to a new day with brightness, or is your thinking clouded by yesterday's remains or today's chores?

3. What did you think about, first thing this morning?

4. Read Lamentations 3:19-23. What new compassion did God give to you this morning?

5. Think of those who carry with them an aura of gloom. (Picture Pigpen in the cartoon series *Charlie Brown*. No matter where he goes, a cloud of dust surrounds him.) Can you think of a time when you knowingly or unknowingly spread a layer of gloom through your home, office, or school room?

6. Read Proverbs 31:25. Have you laughed yet today? How about yesterday? Or the day before?

7. God wants his children to be people of gladness. Read 1 Peter 1:8-9.

"He seldom reflects
on the days of his life,
because God keeps him
occupied with
gladness of heart."

—Ecclesiastes 5:20

# 2
# *But Why Not?*

We all have images of gray-haired grandparents rocking on the front porch, drinking lemonade, and telling stories of the old days—tales of hardships or even good times. What they are doing is comparing the present to the past. While we may not tell the same stories, don't we do our share of comparing? Jobs are more difficult to find, houses are more expensive to build, and health insurance premiums are now sky high.

People change, too. We remember when John was a patient, dependable person, but now he hardly ever listens. Aunt Sally used to be a trusted confidante, but now we hardly ever see each other. Our employers used to honor loyalty, but now the bottom line is all that matters. Solomon advises us to avoid dwelling on the events or circumstances of the past. Such brooding may diminish or eliminate any chance we have for gladness. Solomon says, "Let it go."

But why? The second half of Ecclesiastes 5:20 gives us the answer: "...because God keeps him occupied with gladness of heart."

As we'll see later on, God is working constantly to keep us occupied in him, so much so that we will be fully enveloped in his gladness. We'll have little time or inclination to dwell on the past.

However, what happens when we ignore the first half of the verse? Perhaps we believe we have the spiritual fortitude to reflect on and wallow in the past and still make room for God's occupation. After all, aren't scientists constantly telling us that a large portion of the human brain sits idle? Isn't there enough room in those heads of ours to harbor the good and the bad, the positive and the negative, the glad and the gloom?

Not if you want to learn the secret of gladness. You see, the bad, negative, and gloom are like cancer cells in the head and heart. Once they start multiplying, they eat away at the good, positive, and glad. They take over, crowding out the glad cells. They will eventually kill the good cells.

Satan and his malignant discontentment have to be removed from our heads and hearts or else we will not have room for the Spirit and his gift of peace, joy, and gladness. Paul uses the verb "cleanse:"

> In a large house there are articles not only of gold and silver, but also of wood and clay; some are for noble purposes and some for ignoble. If a man cleanses himself from the latter, he will be an instrument for noble purposes, made holy, useful to the Master and prepared to do any good work (2 Timothy 2:20-21).

"If a man cleanses..." In this case we have to purge ourselves of grudges, thoughts of revenge, bitterness, and sin in order for the Spirit to have room to work, and to create space for God's occupation. This cleansing will make us holy, allowing God to fulfill his purposes and give us his gladness. God loves us enough to allow us to choose him. And we can't ask him to come in until we make room for him—heart-room.

Perhaps we invited God in, but we then encountered a trial and consequently allowed a black cloud of bitterness to cover his Spirit like a blanket. A cloud of sin. Or a cloud of vengeance. A cloud of hate. These clouds grow into a thunderstorm, and soon bitter raindrops are pelting at the Spirit of God, driving him into the recesses of our heart. They cannot co-exist: the Spirit and bitterness; the Spirit and vengeance; the Spirit and sin. God wants to remain in our hearts, however our bitterness, vengeance, and sin may cause us to squeeze him out. As Paul explains in Galatians 5:16-17:

> So I say, live by the Spirit, and you will not gratify the desires of the sinful nature. For the sinful nature desires what is contrary to the Spirit, and the Spirit what is contrary to the sinful nature. They are in conflict with each other, so that you do not do what you want.

Envision a picture-perfect bowl of fruit-plump grapes, ripe bananas, lush, red apples. The bowl is brimming and beautiful. Suddenly someone shoves a rotten orange right into the center of the bowl. A cluster of grapes is thrust up and over one side of the bowl. A juicy pear tumbles out the back. Then, moldy strawberries are shoved into every corner and crevice, in between the peach and the grapefruit, the cherries and the plums. More good fruit is forced out, falling to the floor where it lies bruised. Other pieces of good fruit are contaminated by the smelly, rotten fruit. A once-fresh peach shrivels and shrinks as mold multiplies. Before we know it, the beautiful bowl now holds rotten, useless, unrecognizable pieces of fruit.

Simply put, there's not room for both.

What do you need to let go? What is taking up good space in your heart? Is it a combination of little things, like the moldy strawberries? Letting these go could be as simple as giving yourself a good talking-to, taking a deep breath, or shaking it off. You realize that God never promised an easy earthly life, and the worries of this life—schedules, bills, career climbing—can no longer be allowed to occupy heart-room. So you put them in their proper place. As we'll discuss in Chapter 9, we deal with these matters, we don't dwell on them.

Or, your heart is occupied with resentment, and you decide to flush out the petty cobwebs. So you forget about the thank-you note your niece did not send you for the graduation gift you purchased for her. Or you realize wearing your feelings on your sleeves may have caused more than one unpleasant family scene. You tell yourself to quit glaring at your little neighbor boy every time he rides his bike, remembering how he rode that same bicycle through your flowerbed two years ago. Or you set free long-harbored thoughts such as, "He wasn't there when I needed him last year, so he needn't bother ever asking for my help," and "Turnabout is fair play, right?"

I'm afraid, however, some of us have bigger barriers to break down, walls built by events which have pierced us down to our very core. A simple shrug of the shoulders will not keep us from reflecting on these days of our lives. The only way to avoid reflecting on this type of pain is to reach deep into our souls and forgive—whether ourselves or others.

I'm not going to pretend that true forgiveness is easy. I did not understand how indisputably challenging forgiveness could be until about one year ago, when my husband was hurt. Details aside, let me assure you our hearts were broken, as were the hearts of many of our family and friends. It was very difficult to see my husband in emotional pain, and I have struggled greatly with my feelings toward those few involved. I no longer cared to be around them. Worse, I no longer respected them. These negative feelings also made me feel badly about myself. Did these emotions constitute sin? Through much study I came to realize that losing respect is not synonymous with sin. I learned it is all right to disagree, even vehemently, with someone.

However, it is not all right to harbor bitterness in your heart. It is not all right to cease loving the souls of those who have caused you pain. It is not all right to rejoice when they encounter injustices of their own, and it is not all right to turn your back on them if they are in need. As a child of God, I have no choice but to forgive those who hurt my husband, even if they don't feel the need for forgiveness.

But why? Because bitterness, which grows out of my refusal to forgive, takes up good space in my heart. More than that, God is continually forgiving me. If my Creator does not hold grudges and goes so far as to wipe my sins from his memory, who am I to keep record of the sins of others, or my own sins? When I sin and have asked for forgiveness, God responds. This sin is no more. I now have the freedom to let go of any guilt or burden resulting from a past sin.

If I choose to wallow in the memory of my past sin, I may paralyze my spiritual growth and unknowingly keep God from occupying me. In the same light, if I choose to focus on someone else's sin, whether it be in the form of judgement or harboring bitterness, I cripple my spiritual growth by pushing God and his Spirit out of my heart. Remember, God and my grudges cannot coexist.

God's example and words about forgiveness are powerful. Read the parable of the unmerciful servant in Matthew 18. The story concludes with Jesus' words, "This is how my heavenly Father will treat each of you unless you forgive your brother from your heart" (Matthew 18:35).

The servant who refused to forgive was thrown in jail and tortured.

Countless other verses remind us of the centrality of God's forgiveness and our consequent need to forgive others:

> "And when you stand praying, if you hold anything against anyone, forgive him, so that your Father in heaven may forgive your sins" (Mark 11:25).

> "Bear with each other and forgive whatever grievances you may have against one another. Forgive as the Lord forgave you" (Colossians 3:13).

> "Be kind and compassionate to one another, forgiving each other, just as in Christ God forgave you" (Ephesians 4:32).

> "I have swept away your offenses like a cloud, your sins like the morning mist" (Isaiah 44:22a).

In the Lord's Prayer, Jesus presents forgiveness as a daily undertaking. "Forgive us our debts, as we also have forgiven our debtors" (Matthew 6:12).

God forgives and forgives and forgives all my sins. He gently reminds me that I must do the same to others if I want his forgiveness to continue. Rather than dwelling on how I've been wronged, I focus on how I've wronged God and in turn revel in the glory of his forgiveness of me. If I reflect on God's continual pardon of me, I will not find it so difficult to forgive others. I will realize that as a child of God, I simply have no choice. Jesus said it himself:

> For if you forgive men when they sin against you, your heavenly Father will also forgive you. But if you do not forgive men their sins, your Father will not forgive your sins (Matthew 6:14-15).

Some of Jesus' last words during his crucifixion spoke of forgiveness. "Father, forgive them, for they do not know what they are doing..." (Luke 23:34). Perhaps some of our last words before our heads hit the pillow at night should be words of forgiveness. Forgiving ourselves. Forgiving others.

Get rid of any rotten fruit in your heart that is taking up your Spirit space. If you're not sure what qualifies as rotten fruit, open your Bible concordance and look under the word "sin." Take Galatians 5:19-21, for example:

> The acts of the sinful nature are obvious: sexual immorality, impurity and debauchery; idolatry and witchcraft; hatred, discord, jealousy, fits of rage, selfish ambition, dissensions, factions and envy; drunkenness, orgies, and the like. I warn you as I did before, that those who live like this will not inherit the kingdom of God.

As I mentioned before, cleansing a heart of deep-rooted bitterness is not an easy task for us to complete. But God, being the wonderful, loving, all-providing God that he is, did not just say "cleanse," and drop the matter. As we'll discover in the next chapter, God has given us a Gift who will do the cleansing for us.

# *Study Guide*

1. Is your life easier or more difficult than it was five years ago?

2. If easier, have you praised God for the positive changes? If more difficult, how have you adjusted, mentally, to the more challenging path?

3. Define true forgiveness.

4. Read God's words in Isaiah 43:25. How can we act out true forgiveness? One example may be resisting the urge to remind someone of a past sin.

5. Is it more difficult for you to recognize your own sin or the sins of others? Read Matthew 7:1-5

6. Think of the catch-all closet in your home or the junk drawer at your office. If you wanted to fill that closet or drawer with breakable items or important papers, what would you need to do first?

7. Do you have heart-room for God, or do you need to do some spiritual cleansing? If so, talk about one piece of bad fruit that has kept you from God in the past, or is keeping you from God today.

# *Gladness, Step-by-Step*

I. Seldom reflect on the changeless past.
   **A. Realize that one heart cannot house both gladness and gloom.**

"He seldom reflects
on the days of his life,
because God keeps him
occupied with
gladness of heart."

—Ecclesiastes 5:20

# 3
# But How?

S o there's the "why" of seldom reflecting:
Dwelling on the bad leaves no time, or room,
for reveling in the good, i.e., gladness. But what
about the "how"? How do I refrain from reliving
every detail, picking apart every word, analyzing
every expression my enemy made? How do I keep
from wallowing in the unfairness of it all? How do I
escape from a sin that is holding my heart captive?
How do I keep from poisoning my time with family
and friends, dispensing a piteous mood rather than
radiating the joy of Christ? How do I keep bitterness
out of my head and heart, out of my words and my
expressions?

I've got great news. You and I don't have to!
As children of God we've got the Holy Spirit to do it
for us! The Holy Spirit is the active, powerful Spirit
of God Almighty who entered our hearts the day
we were baptized into Christ. We can use the Spirit's
energy, the Spirit's resolve, the Spirit's strength. We
have the Spirit's power to forgive, to purge sin and
bitterness, and to utter prayers of sincerity on behalf
of our enemies.

Perhaps we've forgotten about the Spirit
within. Maybe Stephen was speaking to us when he
remembered the words of the prophet Isaiah, "You
stiff-necked people, with uncircumcised hearts and

ears. You are just like your fathers: You always resist the Holy Spirit" (Acts 7:51). Shed any resistance and instead embrace the Spirit, ready and waiting to work for you, to guide you, to speak to God for you.

In the same way, the Spirit helps us in our weakness. We do not know what we ought to pray for, but the Spirit himself intercedes for us with groans that words cannot express. And he who searches our hearts knows the mind of the Spirit, because the Spirit intercedes for the saints in accordance with God's will (Romans 8:26-27).

The Spirit offers an endless supply of forgiveness, not to mention patience, kindness, and gentleness. When we find ourselves unable to prevail over a sin or past inequities, perhaps it's because we've yet to tap into the Spirit.

Take, for example, my ever-ready green can of Comet cleanser. Comet is great stuff. All it takes is a few shakes of the powdery green specks, and everything from grape juice to grease virtually glides off! Comet almost works on its own. But what if I tip the pitcher of red Kool-Aid over on my new white countertops, and I forget about my Comet. I scrub, I scour. I pour buckets of water over the stain that seems to spread every second. I work up a sweat. I curse the day I bought red Kool-Aid. My arm is stiff and sore, but I scrub ceaselessly. Still red! I ask my husband to scour. It seems like the stain is becoming deeper! But then, as I reach way back into my pantry for another sponge (I've ripped my first one to shreds) I spy the Comet! One or two shakes, one or two scrubs, and the stain is gone. Pure white again! If only I had found the can earlier.

Perhaps my can of Comet was hidden, having been pushed behind a tall yellow can of Pledge and a jumbo white bottle of bleach. But the Spirit would never hide from me. The Spirit is a gift. The day I was baptized into Jesus Christ, the Spirit, God's Spirit, made a home in my heart. Peter announced the gift as he spoke to a crowd about Jesus Christ.

> Repent and be baptized, every one of you, in the name of Jesus Christ for the forgiveness of your sins. And you will receive the gift of the Holy Spirit (Acts 2:38).

While the Spirit would not hide from us, maybe we've covered him up. Satan provides us with many blankets to throw on top of the Spirit: bitterness, greed, envy…sin. It is up to us to set a blanketed Spirit free to live, breathe, and work.

Or perhaps we acknowledged the gift of the Spirit on the day of our baptism, but we never opened the box. We admired the wrapping paper and the bows, and then we set the gift aside as an ornament, something to look at but not touch. Maybe the physical intangibility of the Spirit masked his realness; the Spirit became an idea to possess, rather than a power to use.

This gift requires only one thing for use: a responsive recipient. Don't worry about batteries, because the power source is endless: God. You won't believe the power that is at your disposal through the Holy Spirit within you! Do you want to know how strong the power is?

> I pray also that the eyes of your heart may be enlightened in order that you may know the hope to which he has called you, the riches of his glorious inheritance in the saints, and his incomparably great power for us who believe. That power is like the working of his

mighty strength, which he exerted in Christ when he raised him from the dead... (Ephesians 1:18-20a)

The incredible power God used to raise Jesus from the dead is the same power readily available to us. Can that power rid our thoughts of bitterness? Will that power enable us to conquer a certain sin? Can that strength inspire forgiveness from our hearts? Can that power enable us to "seldom reflect?" Without a doubt.

Please, open your Gift! The Gift is from God, his power ready to work for you! Paul knelt before God and prayed that the saints in Ephesus would realize the power within:

> I pray that out of his glorious riches he may strengthen you with power through his Spirit in your inner being, so that Christ may dwell in your hearts through faith (Ephesians 3:16-17a).

Don't just read about the fruit of the Spirit in Galatians 5:22-23. Enjoy it! There's an endless supply.

If you are harboring a sin, grudge, bitter thought, or anything that is killing your potential for gladness, call upon the Spirit within to wipe these blots from your heart. He will do it.

May I give my personal testimony of an active, living, working Spirit that cleansed my heart and made room for gladness?

I worked for months to rid myself of the ugliness I felt inside whenever I thought about my husband's situation. As I mentioned before, he was hurt—deeply. I simply could not shake angry thoughts and constant tears. The combination of feelings—sadness, bitterness, broken-heartedness—was sometimes overwhelming. I believed this event had changed me forever. I couldn't imagine being happy again.

Finally, I surrendered myself to the strength of the Spirit. I'll never forget the day. My son was sleeping in his bedroom. I was sitting in our backyard in a green, high-backed lawn chair, dangling my bare feet in Luke's kiddie pool, the two o'clock afternoon sun beating down on my head. Luke's baby monitor crackled in the background. My Bible was propped up on my knees, and I was reading Ephesians. The words jumped off the page: "...incomparably great power for believers...," "...his Spirit in your inner being...," "...get rid of all bitterness...," "...forgiving each other...," "...as God forgave...," "...be strong in the Lord and in his mighty power."

I raised my face towards the expansive west Texas sky and prayed aloud. I asked God to work in me and use the Spirit to purge bitterness, to help me to forgive those I needed to forgive. I asked God to provide me with his power and his fortitude so I could glorify him in my situation. I pleaded, "God, make me forgive through your Spirit. I know your Spirit is in me, but I don't know how to use it!" And then I prayed for those I needed to forgive, asking God to bless them. I named names and I asked God to give them specific blessings. I thanked God for his Spirit, the Holy Spirit, and resolved never again to ignore the Spirit. Following my prayer, I felt a sense of peace I had not experienced in months. I sat there, smiling at that empty backyard, relieved that bitterness no longer reigned in my heart.

Or so I thought.

Months later, I became consumed by my bitter thoughts again. My husband and I were traveling to a Christian conference, and I began to relive our sorrow. It was as if it had happened the day before. As the conference started, I tried to sing, despite the enormous lump in my throat. I was so distraught. I had asked the Spirit to work for me, and I thought for a while that my request had been granted. With a sense of desperation, I appealed to God again, asking him to work through me to get rid of my paralyzing bitterness.

As I learned the next day, my original request had been granted. The Spirit was working in me, leading me his way (not the way I had planned!). I sat through the first of several talks given by a Christian speaker. During the second session we discussed how Christians keep the Spirit from working in our lives. The speaker then allowed time for us to confess to one another the ways we had thwarted the Spirit.

"Confess... Confess... Confess to one another..." The words burned in my mind.

"Therefore confess your sins to each other and pray for each other so that you may be healed" (James 5:16a).

I had asked the Spirit to take away my bitterness. I had asked God to show me how to forgive those who hurt Lane. But what about asking God to forgive me? Throughout this trial I had admitted my bitterness and my struggle with forgiveness, and I pledged to work on it. But I had never confessed it. I finally realized that I had nursed my anger and sadness into bitterness, which is sin. And this sin was still holding my heart captive. The Spirit was not fully free!

I rummaged through my conference folder until I found a blank piece of paper, on which I wrote a note to the speaker. I simply stated that my husband had been hurt, and I needed to confess my bitterness and unforgiving spirit. I mentioned that I was so afraid that I would live the rest of my life with resentment. I finally acknowledged these feelings as what they were: my sin.

I had planned to give the note to the speaker and ask him to pray privately for me. Going forward to publicly confess just wasn't for me. However, something inside me prompted me to pass the note to the front of the room. (As I look back I now realize the Holy Spirit was prompting me!) The speaker asked me to come forward. He then prayed on my behalf, asking God to scoop the bitterness out of my heart. Others in the room came up and placed loving hands on my arms and shoulders as we prayed. Confession. Prayer. Healing.

For me, "seldom reflecting" was a two-step process. First, I had to ask the Spirit to empower me to forgive others, to eradicate the bitterness I felt toward them. I simply could not do this on my own. And the Spirit led me to step two: confession of my own sin and the prayers of others on my behalf. Confession. Prayer. Healing.

The speaker told us that when we confess and pray, Satan recharges and attacks. Sure enough, just one day after my confession, Satan came after me in the form of thoughts and reminders of my trial. I called on God and his Spirit to kick Satan out of my heart. God did it. Satan may attack again; God will prevail.

As the days progressed I would still think about the situation, but with regret rather than overwhelming, bitter sorrow. In past months, I had analyzed the situation repeatedly. Was it Satan? After all, just after Lane was hurt, an acquaintance familiar with our situation left a message on our answering machine reminding us of the scheming nature of Satan. Or was it God, disciplining and guiding? The Bible speaks of God as a loving father who disciplines and teaches perseverance through trial. Either way, I had to acknowledge that God did not stop it — God allowed the hurt to happen. I now had to let him control it. By letting the Spirit lead me, I had finally put God in charge. He can handle anything.

As weeks slipped by, I no longer questioned "Who? Why?" As long as God was in control, it no longer mattered. As my questions fell by the wayside, so did my relentless focus on the unfairness of it all.

This is not to say I will never think about that sad time or that I will never experience a stab of pain or even a shower of tears when it comes to mind. But sadness and bitterness are two different things. Now this event is a sad memory, not a bitter wrong continuing to plague the life out of me. I will probably never feel at ease with those who hurt Lane. I will always question their method and motives. But, so what? God's primary concerns are not if I'm comfortable around certain people or if I agree with them. What matters to God is that I forgive from my heart. And forgiveness can feel so good!

Isaiah's words took on new meaning: "Forget the former things; do not dwell on the past. See, I am doing a new thing!" (Isaiah 43:18-19a).

Soon, I was — to borrow words from Solomon — "seldom reflecting." And what a relief that was!

Once again, do you need to let go of anything? Bitterness? Anger? The inability to forgive? Ask the Spirit of God to do the work for you. Perhaps God and his Spirit will immediately free you from your burden, simultaneously creating heart-room for the Spirit. Or maybe God will point you to repentance, confession and prayer, again making Spirit space. Whatever he tells you, I plead with you to listen. The Spirit will heal you and give you the freedom to become a person of gladness.

# Study Guide

1. a. When someone close has hurt you, what is your first reaction?

   b. In troubling situations do you let yourself react, or do you pause and ask God to react through you?

2. a. How would you define the Holy Spirit?

   b. Why do we sometimes treat the Spirit as an idea rather than a person?

   c. Read Acts 13:1-5. What was the Spirit's role?

3. People sometimes tend to make things more difficult than they have to be. Think of a situation where you ignored the obvious and made things more complex than necessary (i.e. acting on assumption rather than fact).

4. Have you tapped into the power of the Holy Spirit? If so, describe a situation in which the Spirit worked on your behalf.

5. Read Psalm 51:1-10. Then read and follow the advice of Jude, verse 20. Pause and pray "in the Holy Spirit," asking him to cleanse you of any pieces of rotten fruit in your heart and set you free.

## *Gladness, Step-by-Step*

I.  Seldom reflect on the changeless past.
    A.  Realize that one heart cannot house both gladness and gloom.
    B.  **Use the Spirit's strength to cleanse your heart and head of sin and bitterness, so you can forgive, making room for the Spirit's gift of peace, goodness, and gladness.**

"He seldom reflects on the days of his life, because God keeps him occupied with gladness of heart."

—Ecclesiastes 5:20

# 4
# The Benefits!

The most blessed benefit of "seldom reflecting" is heart-room for the Spirit of God. The very moment he enters our hearts, we begin to sense his soothing, cleansing power.

Before starting this chapter, I put my son down for his afternoon nap. I knew he was tired. The redness of his eyes betrayed him. After all, this morning we walked, went to the park, visited a dinosaur display at the local mall, and read five books. But Luke insisted, in his own special two-year-old way, that he did not need a nap. Yet every moment he stayed awake, his disposition grew more and more unhappy. He cried over little things which would not faze him when fully rested. He threw his stuffed animals on the floor, pushed his books off the end of the bed, and gave me an emphatic, "No!" With a dramatic moan, he flopped prostrate on his bed. This is not his normal behavior (thank goodness). It's amazing how fatigue can transform a happy-go-lucky toddler into a mini Oscar the Grouch.

Most adults have experienced similar if not more dramatic fatigue than my son did this afternoon. Think for a moment of a time when your body cried out for sleep. Every muscle begged for rest. Your head throbbed. Your thoughts were fuzzy, your speech muddled.

And then you succumbed.

Maybe you began by soaking in a soapy bathtub, heat soothing the soreness out of your aching muscles. Then you put on a favorite pair of soft sweats and collapsed into a cozy bed with a downy pillow at your head. And you slept. And slept.

Hours later, you woke to the beauty of a quiet morning. You cautiously lifted your head and realized it was no longer throbbing. You gingerly tested your once-aching muscles. You enjoy the pleasant breakfast smells floating up the stairs into your bedroom. The body, once riddled with fatigue, now sends a clear message to an alert brain. "I am ready. I am rested. I am refreshed."

Wallowing in our misfortunes can do to the heart and soul what sleeplessness does to the mind and body. We become different people, consumed by the emotions associated with the memory, the problem, or the sin. Our hearts grow heavy with anger, bitterness, guilt, or sadness, and our soul grows weary as hope is clouded by pessimism. We wonder when, or if, we will be happy again.

As we'll discuss later, God is striving to keep us glad. Our insistence upon remaining discontent takes actual work on our part. We may not realize it, but we are working against God! Following Solomon's advice will give us freedom from that type of unproductive work. We'll actually feel more energized and less stressed. Our shoulders may even feel lighter, as the burdens which once weighed us down have been replaced by the weightlessness of the Spirit in our hearts.

Odd as it may sound, we will seem to have more hours in our days. Dwelling on our adversities can be a time-consuming affair (phone calls laced with complaints, long coffee breaks where misfortunes are mentally nursed with more negative thoughts). Misfortune may lead us to the ear of a caring friend, and talking through a hurtful situation can be so very helpful. But unchecked hurt may turn meaningful conversation into a downward spiral of words, ending in anger and vengeful thoughts. The difference between releasing hurt and dwelling on it may seem a fine line but it is one that is necessary to draw.

Perhaps you've been consumed with a past hurt. The pain was paralyzing. You had difficulty eating and sleeping. Maybe you even developed ulcers. It seemed as though every facet of your life was controlled by the hurt, rendering you ineffective. Then you turned to God and asked him to empower his Spirit within you to take charge of the hurt. Perhaps God chose to heal you immediately, and what wonderful freedom ensued. You were restored mentally, physically, and spiritually. Or maybe God's timing called for a slower healing process, one in which you grew in faith and perseverance while resting in the knowledge that God was in control.

Solomon knew that by seldom reflecting on our personal calamities, big or small, we create fresh room for the Spirit to work in our lives, opening the door for the fruit of the Spirit to bloom into an attitude of gladness. Previous burdens—and all the mental and physical energy expended in carrying a burden—would be lifted.

Unmasked irritation, debilitating fatigue, and spiritual lethargy are soothed into nothingness as we embrace the rest, refreshment, and rejuvenation of a cleansing spirit.

In a couple of chapters we'll discover what God's occupation entails. The fruits of his occupation encompass every good and perfect gift, from the fragrance of spring's first flowers to the successful outcome of touch-and-go surgery, to the awesomeness of eternity. Focusing on our unpleasantries disables us from fully enjoying these and countless other gifts from God.

When I was in fifth grade I became a permanent front row student. I would sit on the edge of my chair and squint as hard as I could at the chalkboard, trying to decipher the fuzzy words and phrases printed in yellow chalk. When I mentioned this to my mom, she immediately scheduled an eye appointment. Within days, I was fitted for glasses. I'll never forget driving down Manchester Road and reveling in the clarity of the scenery.

"Mom, I can see individual leaves on trees," I said. Light no longer blurred; it glittered. When we commit to "seldom reflecting", the blessings of God are no longer blurs, but sparkles.

As wonderful as all this sounds, I've yet to mention the best benefit of all. When we decide to "seldom reflect" on the changeless past and we ask the Spirit to cleanse our hearts, we now have room to invite God's Spirit in to be a permanent resident. Or, maybe God's Spirit was buried in our hearts, and through the cleansing we've unleashed his power. That power is now free to live in us, guide us, and work through us to fulfill the purposes of God every hour of every day. What an exciting thought! The Spirit of God working in me.

This presence of God in our hearts is the foundation for gladness. By foundation, I mean a permanent, rock-solid foundation. Flowers make temporary splashes of color, and rainbows fade, but the Spirit of God will take permanent possession of your heart, if you will let him.

> Do you not know? Have you not heard? *The Lord is the everlasting God,* the Creator of the ends of the earth. *He will not grow tired or weary,* and his understanding no one can fathom. He gives strength to the weary and increases the power of the weak. Even youths grow tired and weary, and young men stumble and fall; but those who hope in the Lord will renew their strength. They will soar on wings like eagles; they will run and not grow weary, they will walk and not be faint (Isaiah 40:28-31; emphases mine).

Let's not delay in asking God and his Spirit to come in and stay. Or, if we've been quenching the Spirit in our lives, we need to let him kindle our hearts into living flame. When God cleanses our hearts, they are ready for his re-occupation. If left vacant too long, Satan will begin planting his seeds of gloom. But God is right there, and he wants to plant seeds of his own, seeds of gladness. Who will our gardener be?

# *Study Guide*

1. a. What was the last physical burden from whichyou were freed (for example, a large assignment or deadline at work; a home remodeling project; a personal accomplishment such as weight loss)?

   b. Describe how you felt when you were no longer subject to the constraints of that burden.

2. a. What did Satan challenge you with last month?

   b. Describe how you felt when "God in you" prevailed over Satan.

3. Read Ephesians 4:29-32. According to this passage, how do unwholesome talk, bitterness, and rage affect the Holy Spirit?

4. Define the word "foundation."

5. Read Psalm 51:10. Pray, thanking God for working through you to cleanse your heart and become your foundation for gladness.

# Gladness, Step-by-Step

I. Seldom reflect on the changeless past.
   A. Realize that one heart cannot house both gladness and gloom.
   B. Use the Spirit's strength to cleanse your heart and head of sin and bitterness, so you can forgive, thus making room for the Spirit's gift of peace, goodness, and gladness.
   **C. Savor the benefits of "seldom reflecting."**

"He seldom reflects
on the days of his life,
because God keeps him
occupied with
gladness of heart."

—Ecclesiastes 5:20

# 5
# *God Works?*

*R*emember your elementary school days, when diagramming sentences on the chalkboard was an everyday routine? Every word counted. In the same way, every word in Ecclesiastes 5:20 is vital. Notice what Solomon did not say: "He seldom reflects on the days of his life but keeps occupied with gladness of heart." Notice who we'd have to rely on—ourselves. We'd do the occupying, fighting Satan all the while. Thank God Solomon did not pen the verse that way. Instead, he said, "He seldom reflects on the days of his life, because *God* keeps him occupied with gladness of heart."

The term "occupation" may conjure images of war time. We speak of some countries as being occupied, meaning forces from another country have crossed territorial lines. The original country is often in subjugation to the invaders.

God's occupation is warlike, in one sense. The enemy is Satan, who would brag, boast, and gloat if he could only occupy our hearts and souls. However, God is bigger, and his occupation serves to fortify rather than fray us.

God's occupation is by no means halfhearted or feeble. First he invites us to the winning side. Then, he gives us the battle plan, the necessary armor, and our supplies. He gives us fellow soldiers to encourage and strengthen us. And he gives us the ultimate victory. Our job, as we'll discuss later, is to accept his invitation and actively respond to his occupation of our lives.

I learned the meaning of occupation when I had my son. Before I explain, I need to share with you Lane's feelings regarding television. The first big discussion of our married life concerned the TV set. Lane did not want one — ever. However, I was a newspaper reporter, and I convinced him of my need to keep informed via local and national newscasts. So, I won, in a manner of speaking.

However, regulating our television viewing has become a way of life. We declare no-TV days and have developed strategies for minimum viewing, like turning the set off after one carefully-chosen program rather than allowing it to stay on indefinitely.

Now that we have a child, Lane has renewed his limited-media campaign. We decided to keep the set, for the sake of home movies and children's videos. So when Luke has watched *Lion King*, and the TV goes off for the afternoon, it's my job to keep him occupied. And believe me, it's a job. I work ... come to think of it, I even sweat! I run back and forth, playing chase, retrieving balls, picking up crayons, pouring drinks, wiping up spills, reading books, chalking the sidewalk, rinsing little paint brushes, cleaning hands, and preparing food. Luke is my child. I love him and want to occupy his time with activities which will bring him joy, knowledge, and security.

I am God's child. God loves me and wants to occupy me, my time, my thoughts, my attitude, my actions, my heart, my words, and my expressions.

"...for it is God who works in you to will and to act according to his good purpose" (Philippians 2:13).

"He tends his flock like a shepherd: He gathers the lambs in his arms and carries them close to his heart; he gently leads those that have young" (Isaiah 40:11).

"For we are God's workmanship, created in Christ Jesus to do good works, which God prepared in advance for us to do" (Ephesians 2:10).

Notice the action words in the above passages: works, will, act, tends, gathers, carries, leads, prepared. God is alive, active, and determined to keep us occupied with gladness! He does not rest on his throne and think to himself, "Hmm, I hope Julie is glad today." He occupies us by working through us to carry out his divine purposes, carrying us close to his heart and planting his gladness in our lives.

This is not to say life is always a rose garden, because it isn't. The thorns and thistles of life that we all inevitably encounter, do not hamper God's continual efforts to occupy us with gladness. In these times, God occupies us with his strength. (See Chapter 12)

God's occupation is not of a general nature. He does not regard you as part of a conglomerate, to be blessed with good weather every Monday, a nice home at age 37 and stress-free old age. No, God is an individualist. If you don't believe me, check out Psalm 139. It begins:

O LORD, you have searched me and you know me. You know when I sit and when I rise; you perceive my thoughts from afar. You discern my going out and my lying down; you are familiar with all my ways. Before a word is on my tongue you know it completely, O LORD (Psalm 139: 1-4).

We recently tasted a physical fruit of God's direct occupation of our lives. Within the last month, our son has been to the hospital for three separate tests regarding his heart. A few months earlier, Luke's pediatrician detected a heart murmur. On a subsequent visit, the doctor heard the murmur again and advised us to investigate. She ordered an electrocardiogram, which showed an abnormality. The pediatrician then referred us to a heart specialist, who ordered an echocardiogram. Lane and I followed the doctor's advice to the letter. We did not think about the cost of the tests—except to give insurance information to the hospital. When it comes to the health of your child, money doesn't seem so important.

The afternoon following the last heart test, we were waiting for the pediatric cardiologist to call to tell us whether heart surgery would be necessary. I could hardly look at Luke without crying. Lane and I sat together at the kitchen table, leafing through a stack of mail, waiting for the phone to ring. I came across an envelope without a return address, post-marked "Nashville, TN." As I opened the envelope, a money order floated onto the tablecloth. Confused, I hurriedly read the words typed plainly on a piece of white paper: "And my God will meet all your needs according to His glorious riches in Christ Jesus" (Philippians 4:19). There was no signature. The money order was for $250.00—the exact amount of Luke's medical deductible. Lane and I were baffled. I had a childhood friend who now lives in

Nashville, but we'd long since lost touch. I searched my memory bank for a shred of a hint. Who could've done this?

Lane told me, "Julie, God did it. This person went to great lengths to hide his or her identity. This person wants the glory to go to God. So let's thank him."

Too many things fell into perfect place for this to have just happened. For instance, at the time I was five months pregnant with our second child, and we had limited maternity coverage. Luke's unexpected medical bills came at a less-than-convenient time. This check eased our financial burden.

The check happened to arrive when we were waiting for the doctor to call with news about our son's heart. Our emotions were tense, and this evidence of God's care touched our hearts. Who else could orchestrate such specific timing?

The check could have been written for a more general amount, say, $100.00, or $300.00. Instead, the figure was exactly the same as Luke's deductible.

God did it. He knew the need. He knew the specifics of the situation. He reached out to us through someone else. Perhaps this person did not even know Luke was having medical tests. How could this person have known the precise moment the mail would be delivered? I thank God for this gift. I also thank God for this one who made a personal sacrifice and allowed himself or herself to be used by God.

The best news of all is that Luke's abnormality, which involves one of the electrical impulses of his heart, is not affecting the functioning of the heart, so treatment is not necessary. We are richly blessed.

God knows the specifics of your life, as well. He is poignantly aware of our needs, our hearts, and our souls. If we are open to him, he will invade.
Let the occupation begin!

# Study Guide

1. a. Imagine a saint arrives on your doorstep and tells you, "I'm here to occupy your home. I'll purify your pipes, cleanse your drains, shampoo your carpets, and dust the mini-blinds." Or, this person meets you at work and says, "I'll reshape office morale, balance the budget, and purge your computers of viruses." How would you respond? Would you welcome the occupation?

   b. Even in the most positive of circumstances, how difficult is it to let someone else invade our space?

2. a. Describe your personal relationship with God.

   b. Do you honestly believe God knows you, down to the depths of your soul? That he is aware of your needs, strengths and weaknesses? Read Psalms 7:9.

3. a. Whom do you love most on this earth?

   b. To what lengths do you go to secure that person's well-being?

   c. Compare this type of love to the intensity of God's love for you. Read 1 John 3:1.

4. Read Ephesians 6:10-11. Discuss the mind of Satan.

5. Discuss a specific time in your life where you knew beyond the shadow of a doubt that God worked on your behalf.

# Gladness, Step-by-Step

I. Seldom reflect on the changeless past.
   A. Realize that one heart cannot house both gladness and gloom.
   B. Use the Spirit's strength to cleanse your heart and head of sin and bitterness, so you can forgive, making room for the Spirit's gift of peace, goodness, and gladness.
   C. Savor the benefits of "seldom reflecting."

**II. Acknowledge God as alive, active, and working to occupy you.**

"He seldom reflects
on the days of his life,
because God keeps him
occupied with
gladness of heart."

—Ecclesiastes 5:20

# 6
# Occupied with What?

God's occupation is not one of swords, spears, or cannons designed to brutally whip us into shape. Rather, he places in our lives people, places, things, circumstances, attitudes, a Spirit, and a Savior so that he may work through us and keep us glad in him both now and forever.

This is not to say God never disciplines us or allows us to experience pain. Nor does it mean we will be free from senseless tragedy. However, part of God's occupation is a never-ending supply of his strength and fortitude, which we can use to wade successfully through life's flooded valleys. Even better, he'll pick us up and carry us through the waters, if we let him.

Have you let God occupy you? Have you noticed one or more of these lately?
- flowers
- blue sky
- orange-red sunsets
- a child's laughter
- two arms
- two legs
- two eyes
- two ears

- a beating heart
- shelter
- food
- clothing
- friends to laugh with
- close friends to cry and smile and read with and pray with
- jobs
- transportation
- health care
- dental care
- baby-saving technology
- books
- fellowship groups
- schools
- cool early-morning mist floating above a lake
- peace-time
- democracy
- a card in the mail
- mothers
- fathers
- babies
- sisters
- brothers
- grandmas
- grandpas
- cousins
- volunteers
- a smile aimed at you from across a room
- hope of eternal life
- a risen Lord
- a God who shelters, shepherds, loves, lives, and dies for you
- a Spirit who intercedes for you
- the Bible
- the Cross
- prayer
- power — God's power — in you

(You might want to continue on your own piece of paper.)

Did the above list just happen? Do we accidentally encounter health, home, friends, a Savior, or God? James says no. He writes:

> Every good and perfect gift is from above, coming down from the Father of heavenly lights, who does not change like shifting shadows. He chose to give us birth through

the word of truth, that we might be a kind of firstfruits of all he created (James 1:17-18).

In speaking of the fleeting nature of physical wealth, Paul advises the rich to "...put their hope in God, who richly provides us with everything for our enjoyment" (1 Timothy 6:17b).

Notice the words the writers use: "every good gift," and "richly provides."

My husband does not like the word "lucky." You pull in the garage just as softball- sized hail mercilessly attacks the pavement. Your doctor biopsies a lump in your breast and test results read "benign." The flu bug flies over your family without making a rest stop.

"Whew, we were soooo lucky!" I exclaim.

Lane responds, "No, not lucky. Blessed."

Big or small, the good-news moments of life are actually part of God's occupation of us. But do we cry, "What luck" or do we kneel and whisper, "Thank God"?

God's blessings, whether trivial or larger than life, are part of his occupation and should occasion praise and thanks.

Take my fear of getting lost. Lane and I had just moved to west Texas, and we were to meet at our realtor's office. Lane gave me directions (to this day I question them). Soon I became hopelessly lost, alternately scouring each side of a four-lane road for the office complex and watching the lunch-hour traffic brigade weave impatiently around me. As tears of frustration began to well, I spied Lane's big, white '65 Ford Galaxie passing me from the opposite direction. At the same time, Lane spied my blue wagon. He honked, pulled immediately into a parking lot and waited for me to turn around and follow him. The odds of us passing and noticing each other at just the right moment in rush hour were slim. A chance happening? Some may say so. But I say, "Thanks, God!"

God even occupies us in our sleep. It was 3 a.m. that Sunday morning when I awoke clutching my stomach. At 39 weeks pregnant with Luke, it took me a second to roll off the couch where I had been trying to rest. I had been placed on bed rest for the remainder of my pregnancy, due to mild pre-eclampsia, a pregnancy complication characterized by high blood pressure, among other symptoms. To this point, I had experienced little discomfort. However, I knew something was dreadfully wrong. The pain under my ribs was searing and constant. I yelled for Lane to call the doctor's exchange, and we sped to the emergency room. My pre-eclampsia had intensified from moderate to severe within thirty-six hours. My blood pressure was dangerously high, and my doctor performed an emergency caesarean section. Luke was born safe and sound at 5:52 a.m. Lucky for me I woke up when I did, hey? A chance event, a simple case of good timing? No. A classic example of God's timing.

When we ponder God's occupation of our lives, we must be careful not to limit God to the physical daily comforts or enriching relationships of life on earth. God's occupation of us includes our earthly blessings. But as God gives these, he also allows these to be taken away. Jobs are lost. Health declines. A tornado strikes. A friendship turns sour.

We should be thankful when times are good, but we need to look deeper for true gladness of heart. God's occupation is one of depth — depth of love and depth of sacrifice. You see, God began working on our behalf in the beginning and he will continue until we are with him for all eternity.

In the beginning was the Word, and the Word was with God, and the Word was God. He was with God in the beginning. Through him all things were made; without him nothing was made that has been made. In him was life, and that life was the light of men" (John 1:1-4).

Remember our foundation verse: "He seldom reflects on the days of his life because God keeps him occupied with gladness of heart" (Ecclesiastes 5:20).

God knew that pure gladness of heart could not be possible unless sin was conquered. Since we've all sinned, we all deserve death. How could we possibly be glad with death looming over us? Our ultimate fear, our most harrowing nightmare — the finality of death — was conquered by the sacrifice of God's son. "But God demonstrates his own love for us in this: While we were still sinners, Christ died for us" (Romans 5:8). This unfathomable act of love is the pinnacle of God's occupation of us. Fathers or mothers, imagine willingly sacrificing your flesh and blood so someone else can be glad, hopeful, and blessed for all eternity. Unthinkable. Sacrifice myself, maybe. But my son? Forget it!

With the conquest of death and the hope of eternity come freedom from the worries and cares of a temporary world. If we were made only for an earthly existence, then houses, food, clothes, savings, cars, and jobs would be consuming concerns. However, eternity has rendered these cares secondary: items to be dealt with but not obsessed with.

"Now we know that if the earthly tent we live in is destroyed, we have a building from God, an eternal house in heaven, not built by human hands" (2 Corinthians 5:1). What does he mean, this house in heaven? Is it mine? How do I know there will be room for me? Because Jesus says so:

> In my Father's house are many rooms; if it were not so, I would have told you. I am going there to prepare a place for you. And if I go and prepare a place for you, I will come back and take you to be with me that you also may be where I am (John 14:2-3).

You mean I have a special bedroom in God's house — a bedroom someone made just for me? Absolutely!

Not only will we live forever, but we will live with God. Revelation 7:15-17 provides a beautiful description:

> Therefore, they are before the throne of God and serve him day and night in his temple; and he who sits on the throne will spread his tent over them. Never again will they hunger; never again will they thirst. The sun will not beat upon them, nor any scorching heat. For the Lamb at the center of the throne will be their shepherd; he will lead them to springs of living water. And God will wipe away every tear from their eyes.

God may occupy you in a special way while you are still here on earth. He may choose you for a glorious purpose. He may send you to a specific place to share him with a particular person. You may be a chosen vessel. Imagine, God hand-picking you, out of everyone in the world, to bring glory to him in a specific way. What a privilege.

God's occupation encompasses everything: the intricate designs on the wings of a butterfly, the comfort of a good friend, the sacrifice of Jesus Christ, the availability of the Holy Spirit, the privilege of tasting the goodness of God in everyday moments, and the knowledge that we will never die! When God sets out to occupy, he occupies!

Paul said it best:

> May the God of hope fill you with all joy and peace as you trust in him, so that you may overflow with hope by the power of the Holy Spirit (Romans 15:13).

Joy, peace, overflow of hope — all the harvest of God's occupation of our lives.

Well, the stage is set. We've decided to "seldom reflect," we've determined to cleanse our hearts of rotten fruit, and we've extended an invitation to God and his occupation. We've acknowledged God's active role in our lives along with the riches he has lavished on us. But how do we transform these riches — our daily blessings, our God, his Son, his Spirit, and his promise of eternal life — into an attitude of gladness?

How does this heart-knowledge manifest itself through our thoughts, words, and expressions? So often, we are given a good theory, suggestion, or idea, but we are not told how to implement it so that it will bear fruit. "So God is occupying us," you say. "All right. Now tell me what to do. Tell me how to be a living illustration of gladness." That's the focus of the next chapter.

# Study Guide

1. List five things God put into your life today to give you gladness.
   1.
   2.
   3.
   4.
   5.

2. a. How would you describe God to a new Christian?

   b. In your description, is God sitting peacefully simply watching everyone, or is he active — moving, caring, intervening, and reaching on behalf of his children?

3. a. How often do you use the words "lucky" and "coincidence"?

   b. What do these words say about God?

4. Read Romans 8:31-32. What does "all things" include?

5. What is the most important gift God has given you? Read 1 Peter 1:3-4.

## *Gladness, Step-by-Step*

I. Seldom reflect on the changeless past.

    A. Realize that one heart cannot house both gladness and gloom.

    B. Use the Spirit's strength to cleanse your heart and head of sin and bitterness, so you can forgive, making room for the Spirit's gift of peace, goodness, and gladness.

    C. Savor the benefits of "seldom reflecting."

II. Acknowledge God as alive, active, and working to occupy you.

    **A. Regard every good and perfect gift as God's bid for your gladness, from the beauty of a starlit night to the success of a lifesaving operation.**

    **B. Remember God's efforts are not limited to the here and now. His occupation of you began in the beginning, continued with the sacrifice of his Son, and will persist for all eternity.**

"He seldom reflects on the days of his life, because God keeps him occupied with gladness of heart."

—Ecclesiastes 5:20

# 7
# *Embrace the Occupation*

God's occupation of our lives is in every sense a gift—the opportunity for us to be people of gladness on earth as we allow God to work in us and as we prepare for the joy and fulfillment of eternity. But, like the Holy Spirit, this gift must be opened and responded to in order to be fully enjoyed.

We have two choices. We can take God's Spirit and occupation of our lives and set them on the mantel, to be admired but not touched. Perhaps we're afraid we'll mar the beauty. But if we do this, we might as well place gladness on a shelf, as well.

Remember your wedding dishes? Suppose I receive twelve place settings of gorgeous, gold-etched china. I unwrap each plate with exquisite care and breathlessly place the plates in my glass china cabinet. I pass by that cabinet every day, look at that china, and sigh at its beauty. But I never remove the dishes from the cabinet, afraid I'll break or mar the finery. There they sit, and sit, and sit, until someday the set is passed on to a relative to sit in her china cabinet.

The other choice is to actively embrace God's occupation of my life. Instead of treating the china as a museum piece, I decide to use that china for all it's worth. I set the plates on my table and invite my family and friends to dine. We enjoy pleasant conversation, heartwarming fellowship, and peals of laughter.

Suppose you are invited into my home to eat on the beautiful china. You are enticed into the dining room by the aromas of fresh-baked bread, tender roast, rich gravy, steamy potatoes, and apple cobbler. In anticipation of this feast, you didn't eat all day. Your stomach is empty and growling and your mouth is watering. But, as you are invited to take a seat, you politely decline and retreat to the kitchen, to sit alone during the dinner hour. No reason, excuse, or logic. No sense. No one I know would respond in such a manner.

In the same light, no man or woman I know could see, taste, feel, and smell the occupation of God and remain unresponsive. No Christian I know, if given the choice between a life of gladness and a life of ho-hum complacency or gloom, would select the latter.

Imagine you are driving your car along a busy street and you approach a red light. You stop the car. The light turns green. You acknowledge the green light, thinking to yourself, "The light is green now. I can go." But you do not release the brake. You do not press on the accelerator. You may mentally acknowledge the green light, but you won't go forward until you let go of the brake and press on the gas pedal.

Complacent acknowledgment of God not only denies the Creator his due praise, but denies me the fruits of a relationship with God — including gladness.

How do I allow God's occupation of me to transform me into a person of gladness? Embrace the occupation. I actively react to God in me—to every facet of every occupation. I choose to respond with the excitement and delight of a child who can't wait to tear open his presents Christmas morning, assemble the pieces of his new gifts and play, play, play (not sit, sit, sit).

As I open the gifts, I must be sure to remember where they came from. As Moses told the children of Israel, "...be careful that you do not forget the Lord, who brought you out of Egypt, out of the land of slavery" (Deuteronomy 6:12).

Our responses to the gifts of God may be varied, depending on the gift. Let's say we are driving along a hot, dusty west Texas road when we spot a field sprayed with bluebonnets. We pull over, roll down the window, and drink in the quiet beauty. Speaking would spoil the moment, so we whisper a mental "thank you" to the Bluebonnet-Maker. What did this response require? An eye for beauty, an unhurried spirit, and a thankful thought.

One of the most beautiful gifts God gives his children is deliverance—in all shapes and sizes. First and foremost, he's delivering us to heaven by means of the death, burial and resurrection of Jesus Christ. God also makes daily deliveries:

- triumph in temptation
- perseverance through trial
- wisdom in parenting
- strength in moral dilemmas

Responding to the gifts of God requires a yielding spirit.

Every time we board an airplane, we yield to the knowledge and skill of the airplane pilot. I doubt anyone has ever told the uniformed captain, "Hey, buddy, you get us in the air, and I'll handle the landing."

In yielding to God, we're not surrendering to the power of a nameless pilot who wouldn't recognize us if he saw us on the street corner. Rather, we are gladly relinquishing the controls of our lives to the Creator, the Redeemer, the Judge; to the Provider, the People-Lover, the Gift-Giver... to our Daddy, our Father, Shepherd, and Savior. We abandon the controls, not with apprehension or bitterness, but with relief and thankfulness.

Countless verses describe God as a willing guide who has only our very best interests at heart.

> ...he restores my soul. He guides me in paths of righteousness for his name's sake (Psalm 23:3).

> This is what the LORD says—your Redeemer, the Holy One of Israel: I am the Lord your God, who teaches you what is best for you, who directs you in the way you should go (Isaiah 48:17).

Notice, he directs me along his path, rather than serving as a backup guide along my chosen course. How wonderful to have such a willing guide. How tragic to pass up the privilege of following such a leader.

Since I became a Christian, I felt confident God would guide me in a broad sense—through moral dilemmas or life-changing choices. However, not every day is punctuated with momentous ethical challenges or dramatic decisions. In fact, some days are filled with routine living: laundry, bills, budget meetings, inventory, grocery shopping, tub scrubbing, diaper changing, and lawn mowing. Where is God's guidance in these matters?

My friend Amanda unknowingly showed me what a difference yielding to God's guidance can make in day-to-day living, in dealing with the mundane events of life.

Months ago, I encountered a series of mishaps. First, Lane's old car sprung a leak in the radiator. I reacted in a very spiritually immature manner, fretting over an unexpected and potentially large bill. I allowed the circumstance to affect my attitude of gladness for an entire day. A few days later, I began a new habit in an effort to re-energize my prayer life and continue growing gladness daily. Each morning, just after getting out of bed, I would kneel and pray this prayer:

> "Dear God, this day is yours, not mine. Open my heart to your Spirit. May this be a day in which you are glorified. Please lead me through every hour. May my actions and reactions be you acting and reacting through me. Amen."

Days later I was drying a load of clothes when I heard a loud, banging noise coming from the utility room. As I ran toward the room, I smelled smoke. I opened the door and realized there was smoke coming from the dryer. In a panic, I switched the dryer off.

The dryer was broken. The car bill had come just a week earlier. I decided I had two choices. I could call Lane, complain, and again turn one of God's days into a day of gloom for me and my family. Or, I could decide to focus on the positive. It only took seconds to think of one blessing. I often leave the house just as I switch the dryer on. Today, I didn't. Had I not been home, I could not have turned the dryer off the moment I smelled smoke. It is very possible the entire house would have gone up in flames.

As I spoke to Amanda that day, I told her about the dryer and what a blessing it was that I was home—a blessing from God. About an hour later, Amanda called back and said, "I just wanted you to realize how much better you handled this situation. Remember how upset you were over the car? And the dryer will cost more money!" (For a brief second my old self popped up and whispered, "What—more money! Thanks for reminding me!) In all seriousness, what Amanda did was help me realize the difference between the two days. I took control of the first day. I gave God control the second day.

In trying to determine whether or not we've relinquished our life controls, we can monitor our actions or reactions to circumstances or people. For instance, what if we are at lunch with friends and suddenly conversation turns into gossip? If we participate in the gossip, we're living on our own. If we disassociate ourselves from the ungodly talk, we've let God control our tongue. Or we are faced with an important decision—personal, job-related, or even a health issue. If we act as the sole decision-maker, we've taken charge. If we ask God for wisdom and wait for his answer, we've let God take the lead.

Actually, giving someone else control is doing ourselves a favor. The responsibility we put upon ourselves to do it all on our own: setting our own flawed timetable, fretting over our human imperfection and the shortcomings of others, fighting the unknown, and floundering in the midst of uncontrollable earthly circumstances, is exhausting. If you've been doing this—living on your own—I've got wonderful, relieving news for you. The Creator of the entire universe will take charge of your day, your week, your year, your whole life, if you let him. Who could better pilot you and your family? After all, "The mind of sinful man is death, but the mind controlled by the Spirit is life and peace" (Romans 8:6).

Perhaps you have never given your life to God, and you want this life, this peace. If you are reading this book and you are not a Christian, I encourage you pray to God and ask him to show you the path to salvation. I feel safe in saying that any Christian would consider it a privilege to study the Bible with you or point you to someone who would be thrilled to introduce you to Jesus. (If you aren't sure where to go, please write to the publisher of this book. The address is listed in the reverse of the title page.)

If you are a Christian, pause for some self-examination. Who is leading your life? Is God in the pilot's seat or the passenger's seat? How do you pray? Do you find yourself saying, "God, I know I can do this," or "God, your will be done through me"? You may be unknowingly denying yourself the fruits of the leadership of Jesus, who told us: "I am the light of the world. Whoever follows me will never walk in darkness, but will have the light of life" (John 8:12b). How sad to think that in our failure to yield to God we rob ourselves of the light of life. I recently learned a song which made me painfully aware of my sense of self-leadership and my lack of God-leadership.

> My heart, my mind, my body, my soul,
>     I give to you, take control.
>
> I give my body a living sacrifice,
>     Lord, take control, take control.

(Author unknown)

Once you've decided to yield to God, you'll experience a sense of peace. You never, ever, will have to complete any task, make any decision, or confront any situation or person on your own. You now have a life pilot who doesn't just know the way, but a pilot who is The Way.

Speaking of pilots and planes, we can't close this chapter without mentioning one more aspect of travel: obedience.

If you've flown many airplanes, you're accustomed to the two-minute speech the flight attendants faithfully deliver....

"Fasten your seatbelt by sliding the metal tab into the buckle...."

"If you have children aboard, secure your oxygen mask first...."

On a recent flight, I noticed our attempted landing was cut short as the pilot guided the plane back up into the air. He came on the speaker and told us, "It's raining so hard I can't see to land, so I'm going to go back up and try again." I then realized the value of the seatbelt rule, as I hastened to tighten mine!

Let's assume we're on a plane that encounters violent turbulence. It feels as if we are riding a roller coaster. The pilot asks the passengers to be seated and securely fasten their seatbelts. Suppose a passenger opts to disobey the pilot's instructions. He stands up, stretches, and begins to stroll down the aisle. Suddenly, the plane lurches forward, then back. The man falls to the floor, landing full-force on one arm, breaking it in two places. Another passenger rises to help the injured man. The plane jolts, and the would-be helper is knocked side to side, eventually landing on top of the injured man.

Why did the pilot issue his instructions? His orders were in the best interests of the passengers, to ensure their safety and well-being.

As you come to know God through his word, you will notice that he gives instructions, advice, and commands: love one another, practice hospitality, be reconciled to your brother, forgive, give to the needy, do not steal, do not covet. Why is it so important to listen and obey these directives?

Deuteronomy 5:32-33 explains:

> So be careful to do what the LORD your God has commanded you; do not turn aside to the right or the left. Walk in all the ways that the LORD your God has commanded you, so that you may live and prosper and prolong your days in the land that you will possess.

The words "command" and "obey" may conjure negative images, such as an overly stern father ready to pounce on his child at the slightest violation of a rule. However, as the above verse explains, God's commandments are designed to prosper and prolong our days. In his infinite wisdom, he knows that failure to forgive can spawn bitterness and even hatred. He commands us to forgive. Wrecked relationships can lead to wrecked lives, so he tells us to reconcile with our brother. Ungodly talk can sever friendships, so he says to avoid gossip. Lying, cheating, stealing, all lead to punishment, and he warns us against these sins.

Read Romans 12:9-21. God's advice includes honoring one another, being joyful in hope, living in harmony with one another, not being conceited, and living at peace. Each of these instructions will enrich our lives.

Every time you come across a command from God, pause and determine how the directive is connected to gladness of heart. I guarantee you will find a link every time. Remember, we are growing godly gladness. Even if the command seems to cause you short-term difficulty or pain, it will eventually deepen your gladness in a loving God who wants to work through you and bless you. As the Psalmist says in Psalm 119:35: "Direct me in the path of your commands, for there I find delight."

The children of Israel tell Moses, "Go near and listen to all that the LORD our God says. Then tell us whatever the LORD our God tells you. We will listen and obey" (Deuteronomy 5:27). God responds to Moses, telling him:

> I have heard what this people said to you. Everything they said was good. Oh, that their hearts would be inclined to fear me and keep all my commands always, so that it might go well with them and their children forever! (Deuteronomy 5:28b-29).

God's commands are motivated by his love for us, by his desire that things might go well with us, and that we might live and prosper.

What should our motivation be to follow the directives of God? Certainly, we cannot deny that we want to live and prosper. However, by now I hope we've cultivated a deeper motivation: our love for God. 1 John 4:19 tells us, "We love because he (God) first loved us."

If we have not responded to God's love with love for him, perhaps we do not fully comprehend what God has done for us. The beauty of his creation. The gift of relationships. The love of the Redeemer. The miracle of the resurrection. How can we help but fall in love with someone who cares for us, cradles us, and craves our presence in eternity? As we get to know the Gift-Giver and actively acknowledge his love for us, we will develop an undeniably deep love and trust. We will not read his commands because we have to, but rather we will hunger after his word, including the decrees and directives, because we know each phrase is connected to an awesome God who loves and works in his people and wants only the best for them.

When we listen and obey, we are telling God that we love him back: "This is love for God: to obey his commands. And his commands are not burdensome..." (1 John 5:3).

When we follow his commands, we are not surrendering to an impersonal dictator. Rather, we are traveling a direct path to godliness. His decrees allow us to follow him with sure footing, to avoid the quicksand Satan places in our path, and to experience gladness of heart on earth as we journey toward an eternal gladness.

Will we mess up? Yes. Will we slip and fall as we allow a sinful thought or act to cloud our journey? Yes. But God knows our hearts. He hears our repentance. When we call on him to forgive, the sin is no more. When we choose to recommit ourselves to his control, his path, and his decrees, we begin to grow his gladness once again.

If we choose to respond to God, give him control of our lives, and obey his love-based decrees, gladness will well up in our hearts and minds and manifest itself in our daily lives. Our personal connection with God will be amplified; our relationship with friends and family will be enhanced; our home life will be richer; we will be more pleased with ourselves, our words, actions, thoughts, expressions, and prayers. We will lay our heads on our pillows at night with sighs of peace. We will realize that our choice to respond to the occupation of God is one of the best choices we could ever make.

I was walking with a close friend who began talking about her children and the spiritual choices they would make. Debbie's simple illustration touched my heart. Picture God, standing before you, smiling into your eyes and extending his hand to you. All you have to do is place your hand into his. But at the same time, Satan is standing beneath you, tugging on your clothes, trying to pull you down. God loves you so much he does not force you to take his hand. He gives you the gift of choice. Satan uses manipulation and coercion. Ignore the beauty of the hand of God, and you'll succumb to the claws of Satan.

Do not mistake God's lack of force for a lack of love. While he's extending his hand, he's working with all the power and fervor of an Almighty God to draw you to himself. He is yearning and aching for you. God wants you so badly that he allowed his own Son to die for you so you could have the opportunity to live with him forever.

## *Study Guide*

1.  a. What is the best present (birthday, Christmas) you've ever received?

    b. How did you feel when you first laid eyes on this wonderful gift? Could you contain your excitement?

    c. Imagine the gift of God occupying your life. What emotions do you experience?

2.  Think of the last big decision you made. Did you pray to God about the decision before it was made, or did you make the decision and then pray the choice was correct? See Proverbs 3:5-6.

3.  Read Psalm 119:33-40.
    a. How are we to obey God's law?

    b. What does the author find in the path of God's commands?

    c. How are God's laws described?

4.  Read the words of Jesus in John 15:9-11. Is there a connection between obedience and joy? Explain your answer.

5.  Read Psalm 119:9-16. Pause and pray for wisdom, asking God to open your eyes fully to his presence in your heart and his wings of protection (Psalm 5:11). If you have a tight grip on the steering wheel, ask God to take control so that you may rejoice in him.

# *Gladness, Step-by-Step*

I. Seldom reflect on the changeless past.
   A. Realize that one heart cannot house both gladness and gloom.
   B. Use the Spirit's strength to cleanse your heart and head of sin and bitterness, so you can forgive, thus making room for the Spirit's gift of peace, goodness, and gladness.
   C. Savor the benefits of "seldom reflecting."


II. Acknowledge God as alive, active, and working to occupy you.
   A. Regard every good and perfect gift as God's bid for your gladness, from the beauty of a starlit night to the success of a lifesaving operation.
   B. Remember God's efforts are not limited to the here and now. His occupation of you began in the beginning, continued with the sacrifice of his Son, and will persist for all eternity.

III. **Embrace the occupation of God.**
   A. **Respond with the intensity of a child eager to open a pile of packages.**
   B. **Invite God to take control of your life, while you assume passenger status.**
   C. **Commit to obey God's love-based decrees.**

"He seldom reflects
on the days of his life,
because God keeps him
occupied with
gladness of heart."

—Ecclesiastes 5:20

# 8

# Get to Know the Gift-Giver

*C*ongratulations! You've chosen God and gladness. What you've done, in reality, is accept a gift — or, gifts. You reached for God's hand, and when you touched it, he gave you gifts so numerous and bountiful they fell from your palms and fingertips and began piling around your feet. Peace. Joy. Hope. Salvation.

Gladness begins to grow when we choose to respond to this bounty — to revel in the beauty of his actions, sacrifice, and love.

Have you ever seen a baby show his love for his mother? She walks into the room and the baby's face glows; he laughs with sheer joy at the mere sight of her. His eyes follow her movement around the room; the softness of her voice thrills him. The baby knows her by sight, smell, sound, and taste. She is the gift-giver: nourishment, warmth, security, laughter, freshness. As the baby grows into toddlerhood, childhood, and adulthood, he will come to know that each gift she gives is motivated and inspired by a special kind of love. Then the love, too, becomes one of the gifts. Unconditional, undaunted, unending.

Each gift from God, from his Spirit to the material blessings to the preciousness of his Son and the hope of eternity, is inspired by an intense love for you and me. This type of intensity surpasses that protective love you and I have for our babies, our mates, our parents, or our friends. The love becomes the greatest of all the gifts, the root of every other gift. Paul depicts this type of love to the Ephesians:

> And I pray that you, being rooted and established in love, may have power together with all the saints, to grasp how wide and long and high and deep is the love of Christ, and to know this love that surpasses knowledge — that you may be filled to the measure of all the fullness of God (Ephesians 3:17b-19).

If we are to experience God's fullness, then we must get to know God intimately.

We will find him in his Word. We need to saturate ourselves with his words, his thoughts, his actions, his parables, his promises, his hopes and dreams for us. We will become keenly aware of his two greatest gifts: Jesus Christ (forgiveness of sins and an everlasting life with God) and the Holy Spirit (our intercessor, not to mention our source of patience, kindness, forgiveness, and love. See Galatians 5:22-23). As this awareness grows, the gladness of Christ will infiltrate our hearts and minds.

Get to know God. Read your Bible. It sounds simple. The Bible is so accessible. Many of us own two or three Bibles. But why do so many of us struggle with reading these Bibles? We want gladness. We know, in our heads and hearts, that God is the source of this and other gifts. Yet, so many Christians are dissatisfied, if not embarrassed, over how little time they spend getting to know the Giver of all life and all gifts.

If you are one such person, take comfort in knowing you are not alone. Also, recognize you have an enemy who would like to keep you so busy and preoccupied that God gets shoved by the wayside.

Then, take action. Following are three practical suggestions for getting to know God, reveling in his occupation of you, and simultaneously developing an attitude of gladness.

## *1. Find a reading partner.*

After the birth of my first son, my Bible reading and prayer life slipped to an all-time low. Those first few months of nighttime feedings, snatches of sleep, and constant caregiving seemed to fill each second of my day. When Luke would sleep, I would feel compelled to catch up on the sorely neglected housecleaning or on my own lost sleep. I'm not going to kick myself too hard; caring for a newborn is tantamount to caring for a child of God. But I soon realized each phase of Luke's life would occupy time that used to be spent in Bible study and prayer. My quiet time was forever changed. I became alarmed. As much as I loved my little baby, it seemed as though my focus had shifted. How could I combine God and Lane and Luke and give each their due time (not to mention other family, friends, and church)? I knew in my head that God came even before my husband and child, but I was not putting that thought into proper action.

I shared this concern with my close friend, Bev. She had two children and another one on the way. She, too, wanted to spend more time with God. So, we decided we would work together to reimmerse ourselves in the Word. We became reading partners. This partnership has been by far one of the greatest blessings of my life. The rewards have been deeper than I ever expected.

First, I have come to know God on an intimate level. Bev and I have studied books I had glossed through in my yearly Bible reading. I say study, rather than read, because we would discuss the meaning of words, verses, and parables. We would look in commentaries, consult our minister, and discuss spiritual ideas we hadn't thought of before. We were learning about God. We were delighted when our preacher would quote a verse or refer to a Bible passage, and we would know what he meant! No sooner would we complete one of our books then the preacher would use the same text in a sermon!

Our partnership brought with it a bonus blessing. Through Bev, I have learned the meaning of spiritual friendship. Our conversations were sprinkled with the Word of God. We discussed favorite verses, challenging passages, and words that stepped on our toes and hearts. Soon, we were sharing spiritual weaknesses and strengths. We would ask each other to pray over certain situations or spiritual deficits. Our friendship took on a new strength, as our common ground was truly Jesus Christ. Spiritual friends are, I believe, the most precious friends in life.

Let me explain how we developed our partnership. First, we took turns selecting a passage of scripture. We would read that same passage every day for one week. On average, the section of scripture contained four to six chapters. Sometimes, we would read an entire book every day for a week, depending on the length of the book. We found that repetition was an excellent way to learn. At the same time, we wanted to remain realistic. If we chose long passages that we could not finish in one sitting, we would only become discouraged. We found daily reading of manageable lengths of material was best for us.

We were accountable to one another for reading that text. Our accountability was not a legalistic thing. I knew that at any point in the day Bev could call me and say, "Did you read?" Or she might call and leave a message saying, "I've read and here are some great verses..." I wanted to be ready for her call. If I had not read, I would tell her that I would read later in the day. Simply pledging my intentions to another person gave me extra inclination to complete my reading. If I did not read on a certain day, I would explain why. Just hearing the excuses I gave helped me set my priorities for the next day. Yes, I felt a small sense of guilt when I would have to say to Bev, "No, I did not read." But this guilt is the good kind, the kind that serves to inspire one to do better — re-prioritize and start fresh.

We did not necessarily call each other every day (although being close friends, we usually talked each day any way). During a day toward the end of the week, we would try to set aside time to share several favorite verses from that week's selection. More often than not, we would call each other with questions about a certain verse regarding its origin or meaning. Individually, we would keep notebooks or journals of favorite verses. Soon, a third friend, Tammy, joined our partnership. She shared in selecting the passages for the weeks.

Bev and I now live about a thousand miles apart, but we are continuing our reading. She sends me six or eight weeks' worth of a reading schedule, and then my local reading partners and I select the next schedule. Of course, we do not telephone each other daily. Instead, we try to include our favorite verses or passages we want to discuss in letters. I recently went online, and our e-mails are often mini Bible studies. Bev and I speak on the phone about twice a month, and often our conversations turn to what we've read that week. Our friendship remains strong and precious, despite the miles.

Bev and I agreed that I should have an additional partner close by, so I could feel accountable on a daily basis. She continues with Tammy and others who have joined the partnership, and God has blessed me with reading partners in my new home.

Bev and I have shared that when we miss our reading and study time, we notice a change in our dispositions. Wendi, one of my local reading partners, has expressed the same thoughts. We do not turn into ugly people, but we lack a sense of stamina and peace. Our day does not feel quite right unless we've spent a portion of it reading his thoughts, receiving his encouragement, and reveling in his hopes for us. When I am able to study in the morning hours, my reading serves as a welcome springboard, launching me into a usually hectic day with a sense of rightness. I know someone will be watching me, caring for me, and leading me. I know where I am going, and with God's guidance I will not be pulled off course by any curves the day may throw at me. And that makes me glad.

## 2. Creatively saturate your surroundings with God.

I walked into work at seven a.m. one morning and sitting on my desk were three or four thin strips of white paper. Typed in large bold letters were the words, "Turn my eyes away from worthless things (Psalm 119:37)." Later that day Dr. William Gerber, an obstetrician who frequented our office, stopped by, pointed to the stack, and said, "Those are for your television." I taped one of the strips to our TV set. There was simply no way I could watch an inappropriate program with that verse glaring at me. It worked.

If you find a reading partner, or are a faithful reader on your own, you will come across countless verses that warrant underlining or highlighting. Jot a few of those verses down on stationery or an index card, or use your computer and print them out in a special font. Tape the verses to everyday places: the four corners of the bathroom mirror; the back of the garage door opener; the side of your computer screen at work; an inside wall of the refrigerator; on the big can of baby formula or the favorite cereal box; the top of the coffee pot; or on the side of the lamp shade you see every night before switching off the light.

Purchase stationery that has a special verse etched along the top of the page. Use checks that quote scripture. If your budget allows, buy and wear shirts that announce your association with God.

Begin and end your day by listening to a song that touches you each time you hear it — a song that provides you with a sense of God's presence in your life. Jerome Williams and Free Indeed sing a song that speaks to my need for daily peace and gladness. It begins:

> There's a peace that floods my soul when the Spirit of the Lord is in control.
>
> There's a joy no bounds can hold when the Spirit blows a fresh wind through my soul.

> Holy Spirit, flow through me. Touch my heart and there will be — there will be such joy! Such unspeakable joy! Such peace, an everlasting peace! Such love, a pure and holy love! Spirit, have your way in me.

We need to heed the advice Moses gave to the children of Israel as they prepared to enter the land of Canaan:

> Fix these words of mine in your hearts and minds; tie them as symbols on your hands and bind them on your foreheads. Teach them to your children, talking about them when you sit at home and when you walk along the road, when you lie down and when you get up. Write them on the doorframes of your houses and on your gates... (Deuteronomy 11:18-20).

Imagine driving home from a seemingly endless day of mishaps: a flat tire, a less-than-pleasant teacher conference, and an eternal line at the grocery store. You lug bags of groceries onto the front porch and greeting you are these words, carved tastefully in the doorframe: "The Lord is my shepherd, I shall not be in want" (Psalm 23:1). Milk carton in hand, you open the refrigerator door only to see taped to the crisper drawer, in brightly colored ink, "Cast all your anxiety on him because he cares for you" (1 Peter 5:7). You go to wash your hands, and taped to the mirror is the admontion, "Rejoice in the Lord always. I will say it again: Rejoice!" (Philippians 4:4).

After reading these verses, your harried, flustered attitude melts into one of calm strength. You regard the day's events in a new light, thanks to God and his occupation. Instead of wallowing in the bad luck of a flat tire, you thank God you had the means to fix it. Rather than fuming over the teacher's complaints about your daughter, you pause and pray for wisdom on how to handle the situation. And you take back your vow to never return to the crowded grocery store. Instead, you sit down and write a note to the manager complimenting the cashier, who handled a long line of impatient customers in the best manner possible.

When we respond to God by surrounding ourselves with tangible evidences of him, his loving wisdom and advice, our frustration will fade into patience and harsh words will be replaced by prayer-guided speech. These new attitudes are living illustrations of our gladness of heart, which will contagiously diffuse through our minds and our homes as we respond daily to God in us.

## 3. Re-energize your prayer life.

Do you find yourself repeating last night's prayer, or offering God a sing-song of platitudes? I have fallen into this trap more times than I care to admit. To treat prayer as a mundane habit, a ritual, or tradition is to demean the awesomeness of God. Not only are we talking to the Creator of all heaven and earth, we are being listened to by him!

To talk to Almighty God is an awesome privilege. In prayer we are able to have a conversation with our Maker. We are drawn closer to him as we praise him, thank him, call upon his name, request his infinite wisdom, take refuge in his arms, and curl up on his lap. We feel his presence as we listen to him. We get to know him as the loving, listening God that he is. To limit prayer to a meal-time or nightly ritual is to deny ourselves a deeper relationship with our God.

I found I was able to enhance my prayer life by changing my approach to prayer. For instance, I discovered that simply kneeling beside my bed gives me a focus I do not have when lying or sitting. I feel as if I'm approaching a throne room, rather than merely giving God his due talk time.

You may want to start a prayer journal. As time goes by, you can re-read your prayers and see how God has answered them. You will realize how carefully he listens.

Pray some of your prayers out loud. Simply hearing yourself give a burden to God offers a sense of relief. You may visualize the burden floating upward, landing on the shoulders of a caring Father.

As you put some of these ideas into practice, you will find that your daily reading, your God-drenched surroundings, and your prayer life become forms of sustenance. Have you ever gone without food? You may develop a headache. Perhaps your limbs become weak and you crave everything in your pantry. Lack of spiritual sustenance has its effects as well. You become spiritually jittery. Your newfound gladness erodes into complacency or dissatisfaction. Gladness seems to have escaped you and you miss it. And soon, you realize you miss God. The two go hand-in-hand, for to know God is to be a person of gladness.

# *Study Guide*

1. a.List three things you do when trying to get to know another person.

   1.
   2.
   3.

   b. Would these methods work in your efforts to get to know God?

   c. How would you describe your personal relationship with God?

   d. Have you dedicated time to developing, growing, and cultivating your relationship with him, or have you expected this relationship to "just happen?"

2. a. What is the difference between studying and reading?

   b. When is the last time you truly studied the Word of God?

3. Read Philippians 3:12-21. Are there any earthly things which are keeping you from pressing on through Bible study?

4. a. Pause and picture what you have pinned to your office bulletin board, sitting on your office desk or attached to your refrigerator door with a magnet. Why did you choose to display those particular items?

   b. If you could pick one Bible verse to pin to your

doorframe tonight, which one would it be and why?

5.  a. Read 1 Samuel 1-2:11. Would you describe your prayer life as intense?

    b. How did you feel after the last time you poured your soul out to God?

# *Gladness, Step-by-Step*

I.  Seldom reflect on the changeless past.
    A.  Realize that one heart cannot house both gladness and gloom.
    B.  Use the Spirit's strength to cleanse your heart and head of sin and bitterness, so you can forgive, making room for the Spirit's gift of peace, goodness, and gladness.
    C.  Savor the benefits of "seldom reflecting."

II. Acknowledge God as alive, active, and working to occupy you.
    A.  Regard every good and perfect gift as God's bid for your gladness, from the beauty of a starlit night to the success of a lifesaving operation.
    B.  Remember God's efforts are not limited to the here and now. His occupation of you began in the beginning, continued with the sacrifice of his Son, and will persist for all eternity.

III. Embrace the occupation of God.
    A.  Respond with the intensity of a child eager to open a pile of packages.
    B.  Invite God to take control of your life, while you assume passenger status.
    C.  Commit to obey God's love-based decrees.

**IV. Get to know the giver of all gifts.**
    **A.  Find a reading partner.**
    **B.  Creatively saturate your surroundings with God.**
    **C.  Re-energize your prayer life.**

"He seldom reflects
on the days of his life,
because God keeps him
occupied with
gladness of heart."

—Ecclesiastes 5:20

# 9
# The Heaven-or-Earth Litmus Test

$A$s we seek and grow gladness, we discover that our life's experiences, knowledge, hopes, and dreams fall into two categories: heaven and earth. The sacrifice of Jesus Christ, the reality of forgiveness, eternity, and heaven, and the gift of the Holy Spirit are obviously all of a spiritual or heavenly nature. They are also changeless. Hebrews 13:8 tells me: "Jesus Christ is the same yesterday and today and forever." Psalm 9:10 tells me God will never forsake me: "Those who know your name will trust in you, for you, LORD, have never forsaken those who seek you."

This heavenly category is the spring from which our gladness flows—a source which will never run dry. How wonderful, to think I can live the rest of my days as a glad person, thanks to God, Jesus, and the Holy Spirit.

We experience this heavenly gladness as we live an earthly existence. We work, purchase food, clothing, luxury items, or take a much-deserved vacation. Perhaps we receive a promotion. We may win a contest or award. Build a new home, start a business, receive a surprise end-of-year bonus. Win a race, publish an article, get elected to an office. While these things concern our existence on earth, they certainly are not wrong. Rather, each of these things is to be enjoyed. We should thank God for the pleasant experiences. After all, the God who made the air we breathe is the same one who blessed us with our talents and abilities.

However, we have to be careful to keep the earthly experiences in proper perspective. When we focus on our everyday circumstances, we run the risk of turning these circumstances into our source of gladness. We become so happy in our jobs, homes, cars, and accomplishments that we do not need any other sources of gladness. We're full. Meanwhile, we let the Spirit sit idle, pay little respect to the sacrifice of Jesus Christ, and keep God at a comfortable distance. We may thank him now and then for the job, car, or house, but our relationship with him stays on a superficial level. This process — letting earthly circumstances displace our heavenly mindset — may be so subtle we may not realize the transformation is taking place.

Too often we become aware of what we've done when our earthly circumstances change, or even crumble around our feet. The job is lost. The house must be sold — or goes up in flames. We lose the race. The raise does not come; perhaps the salary is even lowered. Earthly things are temporary. They can be taken away in a heartbeat. Earthly gladness then turns to despair, even hopelessness.

The gladness we're attempting to grow will never be uprooted by circumstantial despair because our true source is an ever-present, ever-faithful God.

> Know therefore that the LORD your God is
> God; he is the faithful God, keeping his
> covenant of love to a thousand generations
> of those who love him and keep his
> commands (Deuteronomy 7:9).

When speaking of a heaven-or-earth litmus
test, I'm not talking about analyzing every single
facet of life. For instance, when I look at a beautiful
white rose, I do not say, "Oh, it's earthly, it doesn't
matter." No, I praise God for the beauty of his
creation. I'm speaking of experiences that have the
potential of reshaping—deadening or enhancing—
our gladness of heart. I'm also referring to the day-
to-day challenges which may chip away at our
gladness, if we let them.

When faced with these situations, let's apply
the litmus test. Is this of an earthly or heavenly
nature? Will this separate me from God? If not, it is
an earthly matter to be dealt with, not a circumstance
with enough power and priority to alter my God-
given gladness.

More than likely, when we apply the litmus
test, we'll realize that we're allowing an earthly
circumstance to lessen or even kill gladness. Let me
give you an example.

As I mentioned a few pages ago, Lane called
me from work one day and told me the radiator in
his car sprung a leak and the mechanic said it might
take as much as $400 to fix it. You would have
thought that Lane had given me news of a tragic
nature. I became short with him, acting as if he
purposely poked a hole in the radiator. That news
affected my entire day. I pored through the
checkbook, subtracting the remaining bills of the
month to see what would be left over for the car. In
other words, I let an earthly circumstance shape my

entire attitude. Had I applied the litmus test, I would not have wasted an entire day.

Will a $400 car bill matter in heaven?

Does a budget crisis change the fact that Jesus died and rose?

No, despite my frustration and anxiety about our finances, Jesus is still Lord.

Sometimes, such trivial difficulties pose a challenge to our joy that is out of proportion to their real seriousness. In more wrenching events, such as death or loss, we may instinctively cling to God and recognize him as our refuge. But when faced with an unexpected car repair bill or a terminally ill clothes dryer, we forget to ask the obvious question: "Is Jesus still Lord?"

We are hit with these minor challenges daily—sometimes hourly:

- My co-worker received the promotion I deserved.
- Someone spread gossip about me—or my husband.
- The boss is crabby—really crabby—and it's rubbing off on everyone.
- I have to transfer money from savings to checking to pay this month's bills.
- Our friends can all afford to go skiing. We can't.
- The repairman was late and the dishwasher still doesn't work.
- My child did not make the team.

You add to the list. Aren't these the kinds of things that erode, or even eradicate, our daily gladness? We become snippish and irritable. The family walks in the door, takes one look at us, and asks, "What's wrong now?" Gladness of heart, which should be emanating to those around us, is blanketed by our fixation on the latest problem. Certainly, such difficulties must be dealt with. But before we let an earthly circumstance affect our attitude, let's ask ourselves two vital questions:

1. "Is Jesus still Lord?"
2. "What does the Bible say about this?"

The Bible will give us the answers we need either in a general or specific manner. For instance, instead of fretting over a money issue (as I did with our broken radiator), we might read 1 Timothy 6:7-8 before reacting to the situation:

> For we brought nothing into the world, and we can take nothing out of it. But if we have food and clothing, we will be content with that.

Or how about Hebrews 13:5?

> Keep your lives free from the love of money and be content with what you have, because God has said, 'Never will I leave you; never will I forsake you.'

When relationships are turbulent, seek guidance from the passages that speak of peace and forgiveness. Read about how God imparts wisdom to his children (James 1).

Continually reminding myself that "Jesus is," and turning to the Bible for inspiration and godly wisdom will enable me to come to know God even better as I seek his will. Perhaps I will be introduced to another facet of Jesus—his compassion, his trust in the Father. Maybe I will come face-to-face with an active Spirit. Perhaps I will realize a sin that was thwarting the Spirit. When I repent I once again feel the closeness of God. Or, I come through a trial with a stronger character, deeper hope, and solidified perseverance. These are the situations which should result in attitude-shaping. I want to allow these discoveries to draw me closer to God, as I take another step towards gladness in its truest sense.

These litmus questions, and the answers you and I will discover, will take us through the minor and major challenges we will face most every day of our lives. We will experience foundational gladness, rather than "every-now-and-then" gladness. More importantly, those around us will notice our consistent attitudes, and they will want to know the source of that attitude. And we can tell them about Jesus.

Obviously, life will present situations which will be more painful then those minor challenges listed above. We will inevitably deal with death, divorce, job loss, or despair — either in our own lives or those of people we love. In the saddest of moments, God is still there. Jesus is still Lord. God won't leave you; he'll pick you up and carry you.

Perhaps this is difficult to see in the middle of a deeply hurtful struggle. Consider Job, who was suddenly stripped of his livelihood, his sons and daughters, and his health. He cursed the day of his birth and said, "I have no peace, no quietness; I have no rest, but only turmoil" (Job 3:26). Although Job did not curse God, he cried out to God and questioned him. He wondered if God had alienated him. But in the end, Job listened to God, recognized his awesome nature, and repented, saying, "Surely I spoke of things I did not understand, things too wonderful for me to know" (Job 42:3b).

Unlike Job, I have not experienced the loss of a child. Perhaps suggesting godly gladness in the midst of tragedy sounds unsympathetic or even trite. In striving to speak to gladness in trial, I looked to two sources: the Bible, and those who have experienced piercing sadness firsthand.

Perhaps Vicki Dell would have penned these last paragraphs much better than I, because unlike me, she has known both the deepest shadows of sorrow and the warming light of God's comfort. Vicki did not want to die and leave her husband and three children. She went through rounds of painful treatment in her attempt to survive. But even in her physical and emotional pain, she was acutely aware of one unchangeable fact: Jesus is Lord.

Vicki died of cancer last month. And not a person at her funeral doubted the joy Vicki found in knowing and loving her God. Vicki knew she was at risk for developing breast cancer; her own mother died of the disease before age forty. From the outset of Vicki's diagnosis, God was her foundation. At one point she asked God to give her five years, so that her three young children would remember her. God gave her those five years. Vicki and her family were members of a loving church community (the congregation where I was raised). When Vicki's cancer returned, church members expressed an outpouring of concern. One Sunday evening following services Vicki and her husband, Chris, invited members to remain in the auditorium so the Dells could offer everyone a medical update. My mother was a member of that audience. She later shared with me Vicki's incredible dependence on God. Vicki took the podium and tearfully asked her church family to love her children. She spoke of how good God was, and then she proceeded to praise him. How? She used one of the gifts God had given her: she sang to him.

# Study Guide

1. a. Recall the last time you were upset to the point of anger. Were those around you aware of your dissatisfaction?

   b. How do you suppose Jesus would have handled your situation?

2. a. Have you ever experienced a string of mishaps—the "when-it-rains-it-pours" syndrome?

   b. Did this cycle of unpleasantness affect your spiritual life?

   c. Did you step away from God or call on him for guidance?

3. Can the Bible give you practical guidance about ordinary challenges? Find verses that speak to the following:
   1. Breakdown in a relationship.
   2. Financial setback.
   3. Unfairness in the workplace.

4. Read Luke 10:38-42. Who was caught up in the earthly concept and who embraced the heavenly concept? Explain.

5. Find an index card and write down the following:
   IS JESUS STILL LORD?
   WHAT DOES THE BIBLE SAY ABOUT THIS?

   Tuck this card in your briefcase, purse, or another easy-to-reach location. The next time you are challenged by a misfortune, big or small, ask yourself these questions.

# Gladness, Step-by-Step

I.  Seldom reflect on the changeless past.
    A.  Realize that one heart cannot house both gladness and gloom.
    B.  Use the Spirit's strength to cleanse your heart and head of sin and bitterness, so you can forgive, making room for the Spirit's gift of peace, goodness, and gladness.
    C.  Savor the benefits of "seldom reflecting."

II. Acknowledge God as alive, active, and working to occupy you.
    A.  Regard every good and perfect gift as God's bid for your gladness, from the beauty of a starlit night to the success of a lifesaving operation.
    B.  Remember God's efforts are not limited to the here and now. His occupation of you began in the beginning, continued with the sacrifice of his Son, and will persist for all eternity.

III. Embrace the occupation of God.
    A.  Respond with the intensity of a child eager to open a pile of packages.
    B.  Invite God to take control of your life, while you assume passenger status.
    C.  Commit to obey God's love-based decrees.

IV. Get to know the giver of all gifts.
    A.  Find a reading partner.
    B.  Creatively saturate your surroundings with God.
    C.  Re-energize your prayer life.

V. Meet every challenge with the heaven-or-earth litmus test.
   A. Keep your true source of gladness in the forefront of your mind as you experience temporary, earthly circumstances.
   B. When faced with a major or minor challenge, determine if the situation is of an earthly or heavenly nature.

"He seldom reflects
on the days of his life,
because God keeps him
occupied with
gladness of heart."

—Ecclesiastes 5:20

# 1 0
# Let the Delight of Gladness Overflow into Thanks

*I*n growing gladness, thankfulness has a twofold purpose. First, we are giving honor, praise, and glory to the one responsible for all of our earthly and heavenly blessings. Second, when we thank God for each individual item, we are reminding ourselves of how incredibly rich we are—enhancing our newfound gladness!

Have your ever prayed a prayer of thanks? No requests, no complaints, no burdens, no fears. Just a verbal thank-you note.

Picture your child coming to you at the end of the day. Her thoughtful expression piques your curiosity. What has she got up her sleeve? What has she done, or what does she want to do?

"Mom, I have something to tell you."

"Let's sit down."

She draws a deep breath. She looks into your eyes and says, "I just want to say thank you for everything you've done for me." You blink your eyes in surprise, but she continues.

"You took care of me when I was a baby, you bought me that big doll for Christmas when I was four, and you let me have three friends spend the night last month. You make my favorite dinner every Friday night, and you always cuddle with me when I'm sick. Thanks."

Then, she plants a gentle kiss on your cheek and walks away.

What parent would not be moved to the point of tears? What a wonderful feeling, to be praised and thanked so pointedly, so specifically. She remembered that special doll; she does notice you make lasagna for her on Fridays. How simply wonderful. She's your child, you love her unconditionally, and you don't need her thanks. You will continue to care for her and love her whether she thanks you or not. But isn't it refreshing to feel her gratitude?

Imagine a co-worker stopping by, out of the blue, and saying, "You seem to brighten the atmosphere around here, and I just wanted to let you know I appreciate it." No expectations. No suggestions of an unasked favor. Just thanks.

God does not keep a scorecard. One blessing, one thank-you. Two blessings, two thank-yous. But doesn't he deserve a world of thanks?

> So then, just as you received Christ Jesus as Lord, continue to live in him, rooted and built up in him, strengthened in the faith as you were taught, and overflowing with thankfulness (Colossians 2:6-7).

> Thanks be to God for his indescribable gift! (2 Corinthians 9:15).

Enter his gates with thanksgiving and his courts with praise; give thanks to him and praise his name (Psalm 100:4).

Prayers and songs of thanks are components of our praise and worship to God. A Christian cannot help but offer thanks for countless blessings, especially the hope of heaven. Our thank-yous to God are for his glory. However, we can't help but glean additional gladness from thanks. Just set a stop watch when beginning one of your thank-you-only prayers. As your list of blessings grows and grows, you'll be overwhelmed by your wealth. Gladness is rooted even deeper in your heart. This verse takes on new meaning: "The lions may grow weak and hungry, but those who seek the LORD lack no good thing" (Psalm 34:10).

Envision a young boy who has received a new baseball card from his dad. It was just the card he needed to complete his collection! He pulls out the collection, places the additional card in its proper pile, and sits in sheer joy, enjoying the number, variety, and uniqueness of his baseball cards. There are so many of them! The addition of this one card cannot help but remind him of all the cards, as each card fits with the others and makes up his collection.

Instead of a pile of baseball cards, we have a pile of gladness. The blessing of another day of health allows us to further enjoy the blessing of family, which reminds us of the blessing of health of our family members, which reminds us of the blessing of our job, which blesses us with money for medicine when we're sick — and the list goes on. Thankfulness should be a natural by-product of Christianity and a vital part of prayer. But I believe we sometimes treat God like a waiter. We have a menu of things we want, and our prayers are more like to-do lists for God, rather than avenues of thanks. Here are some practical ways to cultivate a daily attitude of thankfulness and pave a direct route to greater gladness.

## 1. Make a family blessings book.

In the fall of 1995 I began to seek the steps to gladness. As I studied the Bible, these words popped up everywhere: overflowing with thanks…with thanksgiving…give thanks…thanks be to God…give thanks in all circumstances. I knew there simply must be a connection between gladness and thankfulness. Yet my prayers and my everyday vocabulary consisted more of, "I want this" than, "I thank God for that." I needed a practical, solid way to direct my mind toward thankfulness, thereby guiding my heart to gladness.

In late September, I telephoned my sister, Debbie, who lived in Seattle. We both had computers and printers, but Debbie and her husband had a color printer. I asked her to send me several samples of paper printed with the words "ANDERSON BLESSINGS BOOK." She sent me five or six copies using different fonts and colors. I chose my favorite, and then purchased a clear, plastic binder. Placing the sheet from Debbie in the front, I filled the binder with lined notebook paper. I was able to stuff fifty-nine pieces of notebook paper in the binder. Each page has twenty-five lines per side, meaning I had 2,950 lines to fill. That's room to list one line of blessings every day for about eight years. In the blank area at the top of the first lined page I wrote my foundation verse:

Ecclesiastes 5:20: He seldom reflects on the days of his life, because God keeps him occupied with gladness of heart.

The first two lines read:

**Oct. 18.** Mom, Dad & Luke healthy; shared Jesus with Terri; Dad and Luke played together.

**Oct. 19.** Darrell's surgery good; check came; Bible study with girls (Bev, Carrie, Virginia & Ann).

I'm almost finished with my first year. Today's entry reads:

**Oct. 3.** Blessing of time to read the Psalms and John 14-17; blessing of prayer.

I keep the book on our family room end-table by the telephone, where I see it frequently. And, you know, no matter what type of day I experience, whether frantic, sad, crabby, happy, or ho-hum, the blessings are there. They may be specific events or general privileges. Each line is filled, in tiny writing. Had I allowed two lines, or three lines per day, they would be filled as well. I normally fill the lines in just before bedtime.

This 30- to 60-second activity, scribbling one line's worth of blessings, has a profound effect on my attitude. Complaints resting on my lips, ready to be spoken as soon as someone walks into the room, somehow disappear. In light of the blessings of the day, these grumblings simply lose relevance. My perspective on life has been realigned, as the roots of the gladness of God have taken an even firmer hold on my heart. I've learned that as my morning reading serves to direct my day, my nightly visit to the blessings book anchors my evening in God's gladness.

Share the benefits of a blessings book. If you live alone, invite a close friend to create a book along with you. Share one blessing a week from your respective books. If you are married, ask your spouse to fill in some of the lines. Include your entire family. It might work like this: Dad draws the children onto his lap and asks them to tell one blessing from their day. Mom records them in the family book. Or, suppose each family member has a book of his own—what a family project! Simply creating the books, decorating the covers, and putting them together can be the start of a wonderful family tradition. Each evening, just before bedtime, you can gather as a family, each one filling in his daily line and then sharing it out loud. Use any format you like—colored paper, special pens, one book for everyone, or one for the children and one for the parents. Whatever our method, God will be praised, and we will be glad. What more can we ask?

## 2. Put your blessings to work for someone else.

I could have said, "Remember, there is always someone worse off than you, so be thankful for what you have." But, honestly, that phrase makes me a little uneasy; it's as if I'm using someone else's misfortunes to make me feel better about my life. I'd prefer to explain it this way. When you're in the throes of painful circumstances and thankfulness has taken a back seat to survival, or if your attitude of gladness has been deadened by repetition or routine, then take the focus off of you and put it on someone else. Find a blessing, any blessing, and use it to meet a need. Two things will happen.

1. God will be glorified.
2. You will once again identify your blessed state and become thankful.

I believe in practical examples, so I'll share how this worked for me. My move to west Texas was the first major relocation of my life, excluding college. I left my hometown and my family. I moved into a small apartment while Lane and I looked for a new home. I knew no one. Although my new church family was as welcoming as one could be, I missed my mom. I missed my friends. I missed my old life. Yes, I had my blessings book. And each day I filled each line. But gladness and its partner, thankfulness, were being challenged by loneliness and homesickness. So I had a choice to make-fight for gladness or let it die. I began praying for a solution and, of course, God answered.

I attended the Ladies' Bible Class at my church, and at the beginning of class one of the members asked for volunteers to drive cancer patients to and from their treatments. It was wintertime, and Luke and I were confined indoors due to the bitter west Texas winds. With time on my hands, I signed my name and became a driver. I did not know it at the time, but God was showing me how to take two blessings, time and a car, and put them to work for someone else. I did not constantly compare my life to those of the cancer patients. However, the nature of the activity was like placing my blessings in front of a magnifying glass. After driving a patient to and from treatment, there was simply no way to gloss over my blessed state. I had no choice but to be thankful. The people I was driving had no transportation, damaged health, and often, no family. I had all of these.

Lately, I've been driving a precious woman named Freddie. In the short drives to and from the West Texas Cancer Center, we've shared bits of our life stories. Freddie has been dealt some challenges, cancer being just one of them. Her first husband died of a heart attack at age twenty-eight, leaving her with a small son to support. She had four sisters. Although Freddie was the middle sister, all four of them have already passed on—even the younger ones. I have four sisters who are all still living, not to mention my husband. And I don't have cancer.

Yes, I used my blessings of time and a car to meet Freddie's need for transportation. However, I find myself being re-blessed, as time spent with Freddie helps me forget my feelings of loneliness and homesickness. I look forward to picking her up and learning more about her life. I invited her to our Ladies' Bible Class, and she told me about her church family. She inspires me with her strength and blessed me with her wisdom. I thank God for leading me to Freddie.

# Study Guide

1. Say out loud five things that you have experienced in the last three hours for which you are thankful.

2. Read Luke 17:11-19. Have you ever treated Jesus as did one of the "other nine"?

3. a. Do you remember the last thank-you note you received? How did you feel after reading the note?

   b. Do you have any overdue thank-you notes to write?

   c. Do you have any overdue thank-you prayers to say?

4. List three blessings which you possess that you can use to help someone else.
   1.
   2.
   3.

5. Read Psalm 136.

# Gladness, Step-by-Step

I. Seldom reflect on the changeless past.
   A. Realize that one heart cannot house both gladness and gloom.

   B. Use the Spirit's strength to cleanse your heart and head of sin and bitterness, so you can forgive, making room for the Spirit's gift of peace, goodness, and gladness.
   C. Savor the benefits of "seldom reflecting."

II. Acknowledge God as alive, active, and working to occupy you.
   A. Regard every good and perfect gift as God's bid for your gladness, from the beauty of a starlit night to the success of a lifesaving operation.
   B. Remember God's efforts are not limited to the here and now. His occupation of you began in the beginning, continued with the sacrifice of his Son, and will persist for all eternity.

III. Embrace the occupation of God.
   A. Respond with the intensity of a child eager to open a pile of packages.
   B. Invite God to take control of your life, while you assume passenger status.
   C. Commit to obey God's love-based decrees.

IV. Get to know the giver of all gifts.
   A. Find a reading partner.
   B. Creatively saturate your surroundings with God.
   C. Re-energize your prayer life.

V. Meet every challenge with the heaven-or-earth litmus test.
   A. Keep your true source of gladness in the forefront of your mind as you experience temporary earthly circumstances.
   B. When faced with a major or minor challenge, determine if the situation is of an earthly or heavenly nature.

**VI.Cultivate gladness, which will overflow into thanks.**
   **A. Recognize your blessings in a daily blessings book.**
   **B. Use a blessing to benefit someone else.**

"He seldom reflects on the days of his life, because God keeps him occupied with gladness of heart."

—Ecclesiastes 5:20

# 11
# Fortify & Protect your Newfound Gladness

*I*'ve often heard preachers say that the stronger we are, the harder Satan will work to tear us down. After all, a weak person may fall by the wayside without Satan's help—so why bother? It's the hale and hearty he attacks. The minute you begin to grow gladness, Satan launches a discouragement campaign. I've been hit by some of his arrows.

Don't get me wrong; I've already won the gladness war, because I am on God's side. However, wars are comprised of individual battles, and unfortunately Satan has caught me without my armor more than once. He's even won some fights. It seems to happen on the days when I haven't found time to do my reading. Little things go wrong: I find a bill I had accidentally buried in the catch-all drawer and noticed the due date was 10 days ago; Luke skips his nap and persists in whining that one whine that sends prickles down my back; I make a birthday cake for a friend, turn the timer off so the cake can cook a wee bit more, and then forget about it. Lane walks in and I feel compelled to give him my "I am-not-amaid" speech. I grumble, grouch, and complain. Satan cheers.

Or Satan may attack at the cruelest of moments: a job is lost; disease is discovered; a drunk driver kills a dear friend; a newborn fights for survival. We may question God, wonder why he did not stop such senseless pain, and pray for miracles. Satan holds his breath in the hope that our gladness is superficial, based solely on what happens in our present life, and that we will abandon God and our focus on eternity. Satan isn't picky; he'll take advantage of you whether you face a day of grumbling, or a day of disaster. The attack may be bold or subtle.

If we have fortified our hearts in God, anchoring them in his gladness, we will be able to react to the smallest or largest of misfortunes with strength—his strength. Here are some practical suggestions for fashioning the strength of God into armor to be used for safeguarding and solidifying our gladness of heart.

## 1. *Give God helmet duty.*

When gladness seems to diminish or lose its luster, you will know it. Once you've experienced the gladness of God, you'll never forget it. Rather than relying on yourself to reconstruct your attitude, call on the One who gave you gladness of heart to begin with. Do not be shy about asking God to point you to his gladness again.

"God, Satan has worked his way into my heart. Get him away from me."

"God, I've lost it. I went five days without once picking up the Bible, and my blessings book is six days behind. You are bigger than my to-do list.

Please be my strength so that my attitude will be godly once again. I want gladness."

Kneel in prayer, ask God to re-arm you with his strength, and remember: "…the Lord is faithful, and he will strengthen and protect you from the evil one" (2 Thessalonians 3:3).

## 2. Account for your weaknesses before Satan does, and then build your armor accordingly.

Do you know the phrase, "He knows how to push my buttons?" I know exactly what to say to Lane to frustrate him. I know what words to use, what tone to employ, and what sigh to heave to really rattle his nerves. In the same way, I know what circumstances or moods can give my gladness a severe shaking. I have a thorn in my flesh that challenges my spirituality and disturbs my gladness in God. I have temptations and weaknesses that could be my undoing. I know them, God knows them, and so does Satan.

I'll share just one with you: envy. Nothing can kill my gladness like a good dose of envy. If I leave my envy exposed, Satan will run with it. But God is bigger than my envy. He prefers that I use his strength to squelch it as quickly as possible. I've found two useful aids in my battle against envy: my Bible concordance and a picture on my refrigerator.

When I graduated from college, I found a job in my field: journalism. I was a reporter for the *Abilene Reporter-News* in Abilene, Texas, and I loved it. I looked forward to going to work each day. When Lane graduated from Abilene Christian University with his master's degree, he found a job in another state. I was sorry to leave the newspaper, but I was excited at Lane's success, and I did not doubt my ability to quickly find another satisfying job. It took me eighteen months to find a job in my field. In the meantime, I was an administrative assistant at a car rental agency. The people were nice, but the job description paled in comparison to my former reporting job. During this period, my college friends were excelling in their jobs — all in our mutual field of journalism. Candy had moved into newspaper management. Kenneth was a business reporter. Cindy was in charge of the company newsletter for a major restaurant chain. I was working at a car rental agency.

I was so envious of the success of my friends, and my emotions ranged from self-pity to embarrassment. I did not want to take away the jobs of my college friends; I just wanted one for myself, too. This envy infused my mind and my heart, and gladness was nowhere to be found. Rejection letters continued to frequent my mailbox, as I applied for jobs in my line of work. I was basing the attitude of my heart on my inability to find a good job coupled with the enviable successes of my friends.

Verses like James 3:16 opened my eyes. "For where you have envy and selfish ambition, there you find disorder and every evil practice."

The concordance in the back of my Bible has sixteen entries under "Envy" and "Envying." Often when I'm overwhelmed with envious thoughts, I open my Bible and flip to and from the concordance and the listed verses. They are underlined in red ink. Sixteen verses are enough to build quite an armor. Part of my armor is the sword, the Word, which helps me slice through the envious thoughts that try to pierce my spirit. Satan watches helplessly, as the breastplate of God deflects Satan's envy arrows.

At another stage in my life, I added a second piece of equipment to my envy defense. I had developed a nasty habit of comparing our lot in life to that of others who seemed to have made all the right choices and found all the right answers. It seemed our friends were on their way and we were still three steps behind. I recognized this habit as another form of envy—the thorn in my flesh.

I again read the Bible verses about envy, and I began a turnaround. During that period, I was an avid reader of *Newsweek* magazine. I came across a picture in a magazine depicting two Rwandan children lying by a water well. Their emaciated bodies and desperate faces spoke of starvation and despair. As I stated earlier, I feel odd using someone else's tragedy to make myself feel better. But this picture challenged every envious thought I had ever had. These children lacked the basics: food, clothing and shelter. What right had I to envy someone else's job (when I already had a job) when thousands of children would give almost anything to be wearing my shoes. I imagine that the parents of those sons and daughters would beg for my job at the rental agency. If anyone had the right to be envious, it was those pitiful children. I cut the picture from the magazine, placed it on the refrigerator and told Lane, "Whenever I begin to complain, tell me to look at that picture." The photo was a daily visual reminder of my blessed state, while the words in my Bible reminded me of the wrongness of envy and the rightness of contentment.

## 3. Be a fighter: Shoot your own arrows.

Imagine yourself fully embroiled in battle. You are encased in armor and you stand with your shield deflecting the enemy's attacks. Your shield is body-length and body-width. You are protected, and the enemy does not penetrate your covering of steel. But you do not advance even one inch toward the line of victory. You do not grow. You stand and defend, stand and defend, stand and defend. Envision how weary you'd become.

What if you carried the battle to the enemy? What if you saw victory and went after it, shooting arrows at Satan with such speed that he never had time to re-draw his battle plan? He will always be an avid attacker, but why give him any advantages? Why not advance toward victory?

James tells us,

> Submit yourselves, then, to God. Resist the devil, and he will flee from you. Come near to God and he will come near to you (James 4:7-8a).

One way we can draw near to God and attack Satan at the same time is to obey God by loving others. Paul tells us, "The entire law is summed up in a single command: 'Love your neighbor as yourself' " (Galatians 5:14).

I wish I actually did half of the things I thought about doing. How often do these words flit in and out of your mind?

"I've got to pray for him during this time of crisis."

"I need to send her a card."

"I really should take her kids for the afternoon and give her some rest."

"I'm going to sign up for that volunteer project as soon as I get the chance."

"When things settle down, we'll start that Bible study."

"I know the Bible says I should pray for my enemies, but I must have time to get over my anger."

Every time we do a good work—not just think about it—we throw a dart Satan's way. And when we know of a good work we should do but we lazily, or purposely, let the moment pass, we lose ground in the battle.

James 4:17 reads, "Anyone, then, who knows the good he ought to do and doesn't do it, sins." In the context of this chapter, James is telling his readers to submit themselves to God and turn away from their selfish living.

Doing the good we ought to do does not mean taking on too much, sacrificing family for the sake of others. The unselfish living God asks of us is described in Philippians 2:3-4:

Do nothing out of selfish ambition or vain conceit, but in humility consider others better than yourselves. Each of you should look not only to your own interest, but also the interests of others.

Love is an action word, and loving God by loving our neighbors as ourselves requires thought coupled with action.

Don't just think about your blessings. Give thanks.

Don't just think about a blessings book. Make one.

Don't just think about sending a card. Buy a card, then mail it.

Don't just think about making a meal for a sick person. Deliver it.

Don't just think about finding a reading partner. Start asking people.

Don't just think about the starving children in Rwanda. Call someone in charge and say, "What can I do?" Then do it.

Don't just think about mentioning Jesus to your neighbors when the opportunity arises. Make the opportunity.

Be protective of your gladness of heart—guard it with your life. But do not simply defend it. Advance toward victory. Draw near to God by loving your neighbor, and send Satan into retreat.

# *Study Guide*

1. Read Ephesians 6:10-11.
   a. Has the devil ever schemed against you?

   b. Did the devil come after you during a weak point of your life or a strong point of your life?

2. a. Have you ever lost an important item — a watch, piece of jewelry, or a wallet? Think how fervently you searched for the missing article.

   b. Have you ever lost a piece of your spirituality, the peace of God or gladness of heart?

   c. How did you recapture this gladness?

3. a. Do you have a particular sin or spiritual struggle that continually challenges you, and has Satan tried to take advantage of this weakness?

   b. Read 1 Peter 5:8. Search the scriptures and find two passages you can use as spiritual defenses.

4. a. Is your spiritual life effective and productive?

   b. What steps can you take to continue growth? Read 2 Peter 1:3-10.

5. a. What good is an intention without a matching action?

   b. What can mere intention do for spiritual growth?

   c. Read Ephesians 2:10. Pray and ask God to use

you for a good work and to give you the wisdom and power to complete the work.

# Gladness, Step-by-Step

I. Seldom reflect on the changeless past.
   A. Realize that one heart cannot house both gladness and gloom.
   B. Use the Spirit's strength to cleanse your heart and head of sin and bitterness, so you can forgive, making room for the Spirit's gift of peace, goodness, and gladness.
   C. Savor the benefits of "seldom reflecting."

II. Acknowledge God as alive, active, and working to occupy you.
   A. Regard every good and perfect gift as God's bid for your gladness, from the beauty of a starlit night to the success of a lifesaving operation.
   B. Remember God's efforts are not limited to the here and now. His occupation of you began in the beginning, continued with the sacrifice of his Son, and will persist for all eternity.

III. Embrace the occupation of God.
   A. Respond with the intensity of a child eager to open a pile of packages.
   B. Invite God to take control of your life, while you assume passenger status.
   C. Commit to obey God's love-based decrees.

IV. Get to know the giver of all gifts.
   A. Find a reading partner.

B. Creatively saturate your surroundings with God.

C. Re-energize your prayer life.

V. Meet every challenge with the heaven-or-earth litmus test.

A. Keep your true source of gladness in the forefront of your mind as you experience temporary earthly circumstances.

B. When faced with a major or minor challenge, determine if the situation is of an earthly or heavenly nature.

VI. Cultivate gladness, which will overflow into thanks.

A. Recognize your blessings in a daily blessings book.

C. Use a blessing to benefit someone else.

**VII. Fortify and protect your newfound gladness.**

**A. When gladness has escaped you, go to God.**

**B. Work on your spiritual weaknesses before Satan does.**

**C. Intentionally launch your own spiritual attack by means of active good works.**

"He seldom reflects
on the days of his life,
because God keeps him
occupied with
gladness of heart."

—Ecclesiastes 5:20

# 12
# *What About the Pain?*

*T*he women of our church are getting ready for our annual Ladies' Retreat. We chose the theme, "Make a Joyful Noise." Our speakers will focus on our joy in Christ and how that joy spills over into the various roles we play. The planning committee became excited as we envisioned an upbeat weekend: ice-breaking games, singing, skits, fellowship, study, and prayer. "The Joy of the Lord" will be our theme song. The retreat is two weeks away. Signs and bulletin boards adorn the church walls with the word "JOYFUL!"

In the last eleven days, we have buried five members of our church. We are still reeling from the sudden death of one of our elders, about two months ago. Another elder is battling cancer. A local company just closed its doors, leaving one of our members jobless. I could go on. Are these people expected to make a joyful noise? How can they possibly be people of gladness when their hearts are aching?

Two people answered my question. First, Jesus Christ. Second, one of my sisters in faith.

Our Savior, in the midst of tremendous sorrow and impending physical pain, relied on the will of his father. Just before his death, Jesus prayed, "My Father, if it is possible, may this cup be taken from me. Yet not as I will, but as you will" (Matthew 26:39b).

Jesus was a man. He knew true heartache. He had firsthand knowledge of excruciating pain. Yet these harrowing moments did not destroy him, for he knew his destination. With the crucifixion looming, Jesus told Pilate, "My kingdom is not of this world. If it were, my servants would fight to prevent my arrest by the Jews. But now my kingdom is from another place" (John 18:36).

Jesus had at his disposal legions of angels who could rescue him at any moment. However, his faith and love for the Father saw him through heartache I cannot even begin to fathom.

The second person who taught me gladness despite pain, Mildred Rogers, also has encountered sorrow that I cannot truly understand. In her mid 80s, Mildred is the life of a party. In her 70s, she took a long-coveted ride in a hot air balloon. When she sees friends at church, she welcomes them with an enthusiastic hug and smile. But the last several months, I have struggled with what to say to Mildred as she greeted me with her warm embrace.

I want to ask, "How are you?" but I stammer and stutter instead. How are you supposed to be when you are watching your child die a slow death from cancer? Each time I saw Mildred, I asked about her son, Jerry. Some days she would explain the ruthlessness of the disease, how it had invaded Jerry's vital organs. Other times she would simply reply, "We're living day by day." Mildred was not just hurting for Jerry, or herself, but for Jerry's brothers, as well. She would tell me how her other sons traveled home to be with Jerry as much as they possibly could and how watching their brother die was the deepest sorrow of their lives. Mildred and her family buried Jerry less than a week ago.

During the months of Jerry's suffering, Mildred continued to attend Ladies' Bible Class every Wednesday. One morning I was teaching on the topic, "Contentment." I opened the class by asking the simple question, "Are you content?" I could not look at Mildred, because I felt guilty throwing the word "contentment" in her face. But hers was the first voice to respond. As I looked at her, she was nodding her head and saying "yes," despite the tears watering her eyes. Mildred must have known my thoughts, because she didn't stop there. She told the class, "I am at peace. I know where I am going."

Can contentment and pain co-exist? Can gladness live in the same heart with agonizing sorrow? Mildred would not hesitate to say that watching Jerry die was painful—wounding her to the core of her being. Yet even this sorrow of sorrows could not unsettle her anchored knowledge that Jesus is Lord, and God is love.

Mildred told the class that she did not understand how people without God could live through such sorrows. She spoke of how good God is, and she proceeded to thank her Christian friends for their prayers, cards, hugs, and support. Mildred was not only content, she was experiencing gladness. She told her Christian sisters how glad she was to know a God who would take her through sorrow, and she was thanking her God for giving her supportive, caring friends. I listened to her in awe as she praised God and gave thanks, while the rest of us wiped away tears of sympathy.

Mildred let God pick her up and carry her, minute by minute, second by second, through this valley of sorrow. He was her sanctuary. Perhaps Mildred did not realize it at the time, but she was teaching us the meaning of Psalm 5:11:

> But let all who take refuge in you be glad; let them ever sing for joy. Spread your protection over them that those who love your name may rejoice in you.

Gladness of heart is not a giddy display of emotion: giggles, non-stop grins, and gushing sentiment. Yes, gladness is most often expressed through smiles, pleasantness, cheerfulness, and laughter. But gladness of heart goes deeper. Our disposition radiates our knowledge of God, our joy in our salvation, and our security in Jesus Christ. As Mildred put it, "I know where I am going." And despite her pain, this knowledge made her glad.

Romans 8:38-39 illustrates the unshakable source of this gladness:

> For I am convinced that neither death nor life, neither angels nor demons, neither the present nor the future, nor any powers, neither height nor depth, nor anything else in all creation, will be able to separate us from the love of God that is in Christ Jesus our Lord.

Neither job loss nor illness. Neither tornados nor plane crashes. Neither drunk drivers nor terrorists. Neither loss of a mate nor loss of a child. In these most distressing of moments, the birds may not sing. Sunsets are drab. Flowers seem colorless. It seems almost cruel that people around you can continue with their daily routines in the midst of your suffering. Every ounce of gladness you found in earthly blessings has disappeared. You think laughter is a thing of the past. But still, you are not alone. And you never will be. You can curl up in the arms of a God who will wade the waters, climb the impossible hills, and weather the brutal storms. Never will he leave you, nor will he forsake you. In these moments, this is your gladness.

Please, do not feel guilty for allowing yourself to hurt. The pain we experience as human beings does not eradicate the gladness we have found in our God. One does not cancel the other.

A hurt heart is not a sinful heart. This pain is not the same as those seeds of gloom that Satan loves to nurture in us. Our Savior Jesus Christ also experienced deep pain and sadness. In the Garden of Gethsemane, he told his disciples that his soul was "overwhelmed with sorrow to the point of death." (Matthew 26:38b).

If you are in the throes of pain, I pray that your Christian friends will ask God to carry and comfort you. And as your thinking becomes less cloudy and you are able to eat a full meal and sleep more than half the night, I pray that you will continue to rely on the security of your anchor in Christ. Your foundational gladness in the Lord will see you through the storms in the blackest of seasons. And you will be able to recite your own version of Habakkuk 3:17-18:

> Though the fig tree does not bud
> and there are no grapes on the vines,
> though the olive crop fails
> and the fields produce no food,
> though there are no sheep in the pen
> and no cattle in the stalls,
> yet I will rejoice in the LORD,
> I will be joyful in God my Savior.

# Study Guide

1. a. Are Christians promised a pain-free life? Notice how scripture in general refers to "when you face trials...," not "if you face trials..."

   b. Read Ecclesiastes 9:11-12 and James 1:2-4. Do you know any adults who have lived painless lives?

2. What has been the greatest hurt of your life?

3. a. Explain God's role as the Great Comforter, using verses such as Isaiah 46:3-4, Psalm 55:22, and Psalm 68:19

   b. How did God carry you through the greatest struggle of your life?

4. Try to describe the crucifixion through God's eyes.

5. If you are in the midst of a deep hurt, pause and read 1 Peter 5:7. Ask God to help you cast your burden on him. Ask him to carry you as a shepherd carries a wounded lamb.

# Gladness, Step-by-Step

I. Seldom reflect on the changeless past.
   A. Realize that one heart cannot house both gladness and gloom.
   B. Use the Spirit's strength to cleanse your heart and head of sin and bitterness, so you

can forgive, making room for the Spirit's gift of peace, goodness, and gladness.
C. Savor the benefits of "seldom reflecting."

II. Acknowledge God as alive, active, and working to occupy you.
A. Regard every good and perfect gift as God's bid for your gladness, from the beauty of a starlit night to the success of a lifesaving operation.
B. Remember God's efforts are not limited to the here and now. His occupation of you began in the beginning, continued with the sacrifice of his Son, and will persist for all eternity.

III. Embrace the occupation of God.
A. Respond with the intensity of a child eager to open a pile of packages.
B. Invite God to take control of your life, while you assume passenger status.
C. Commit to obey God's love-based decrees.

IV. Get to know the giver of all gifts.
A. Find a reading partner.
B. Creatively saturate your surroundings with God.
C. Re-energize your prayer life.

V. Meet every challenge with the heaven-or-earth litmus test.
A. Keep your true source of gladness in the forefront of your mind as you experience temporary earthly circumstances.
B. When faced with a major or minor challenge, determine if the situation is of an

earthly or heavenly nature.

VI. Cultivate gladness, which will overflow into thanks.
   A. Recognize your blessings in a daily blessings book.
   B. Use a blessing to the benefit of someone else.

VII. Fortify and protect your newfound gladness.
   A. When gladness has escaped you, go to God.
   B. Work on your spiritual weaknesses before Satan does.
   C. Intentionally launch your own spiritual battles by means of active good works.

VIII. Allow God to carry you through pain.
   A. Realize nothing can separate you from the love of God.
   B. Remember that sadness does not displace gladness rooted in God.

"He seldom reflects
on the days of his life,
because God keeps him
occupied with
gladness of heart."

—Ecclesiastes 5:20

# 13
# Gladness
# and the Body

Mildred explained on more than one occasion how God gave her Christian brothers and sisters who supported her through Jerry's battle with cancer and his death. God placed Mildred in a church family, a body which, when working correctly, is a living illustration of 1 Corinthians 12:26: "If one part suffers, every part suffers with it; if one part is honored, every part rejoices with it." The cards sent, the food cooked, the prayers offered, and the tears cried for Mildred were all inspired by concern and love from others in the body. When she hurt, we hurt.

Today, I learned a lesson in interconnected pain. This morning, our family of four scurried around frantically. We were headed to a local photographer's studio for our first official family picture since Luke's little brother Jake came on the scene. We piled into the car and headed for the studio. I was sitting in the back with the boys, smoothing down stray strands of blonde hair, when I heard Lane exclaim, "What are they doing!"

A big, red Cadillac pulled out in front of us, and there was no stopping. As I tensed up for the collision, I instinctively flung my hand in front of Jake, who was buckled in his car seat next to me.

When we crashed into the Cadillac, my left hand smashed into the back of the seat in front of me, jamming my knuckles and spraining three fingers. Big deal—could have been a lot worse, right? But let me tell you, IT HURTS!

The only parts of my body directly affected by the accident are my left hand and wrist. But my whole body senses the pain in my left hand, and each part responds as it can in order to provide comfort and aid healing. With my ears, I listened to the doctor tell me to apply an ice pack and keep the hand elevated. My legs and feet carry me to the medicine cabinet, and my uninjured hand and arm reach for the bottle of pain relief pills.

One vital body part made these soothing acts possible: the head. My brain coordinated motion throughout my body in response to the need of my hurt hand.

God likens the church body to our physical bodies, and he places special emphasis on the head: Christ.

> The body is a unit, though it is made up of many parts; and though all its parts are many, they form one body. So it is with Christ (1 Corinthians 12:12).

> So in Christ we who are many form one body, and each member belongs to all the others (Romans 12:5).

> And God placed all things under his feet and appointed him to be head over everything for the church, which is his body, the fullness of him who fills everything in every way (Ephesians 1:22-23).

> And he is the head of the body, the church;
> he is the beginning and the firstborn from
> among the dead, so that in everything he
> might have the supremacy (Colossians 1:18).

Just as impulses from my brain direct the action of my body, so Christ directs the actions of his body. My brain told my body, "Take care of the injured hand." Christ tells us, "Take care of one another."

God gave you a special place and put you exactly where he wanted you within his body, the church. What does this have to do with gladness? As parts of a living body, we all share in the life that comes through Christ. We give and receive the gladness of that life as we love and serve one another.

Has Christ's body been a source of gladness in your life? Our churches excel in dispensing gladness through comfort. Before my first son was born I experienced an eleven-week pregnancy which ended in miscarriage. That evening a flower-filled vase appeared on my front porch. Steaming, home-cooked meals were placed on my kitchen table. Forty cards arrived in my mailbox. I received a book written to minister to those who had lost babies. One of our church members had purchased the book and loaned it to each woman who miscarried. Everyone who read the book signed her name on the inside. As I added my name, I read the signatures of members of my church family who understood my emotions. I was comforted over and over again by my spiritual body.

The gladness found in the body of Christ is multifaceted. As Christ's church superbly supplies gladness amidst physical or emotional hardship, so the body excels in dispensing gladness when we pass through trials of the soul.

When my prayer life is sick, prayer warriors will nurse me back to health.

When my shield of faith is cracked, the church will help me mend it.

When sin rears its ugly head, the priesthood of believers will hear my confession.

When my appetite for God's word is weak, the body of Christ will help me remember my need for pure, spiritual food.

I have a sister in Christ who is genuinely interested in my spiritual state. In fact, in almost every conversation we share, Jeri asks me, "How's your walk with God?" When my faith is vibrant, Jeri is happy for me. However, when it seems my relationship with God is on a back burner, Jeri gently encourages me.

Others in the body encourage me to persevere when I'm weary or slow down when I've taken on too much. A wonderful aspect of the body is its diversity. So many parts. So many functions. So many experiences. So many to identify with the flatness I feel when I'm out of step with the Lord. So many to share my exhilaration when I re-discover the compassion of Christ. In the body I will find not only sympathy but empathy. While I hurt deeply for Mildred, I could not say to Mildred, "I know how you feel." But others who had endured the loss of a child could take Mildred in their arms and whisper those comforting words.

At our weekly Ladies' Bible Class, we devote a special part of the class to 1 Corinthians 12:26: "If one part suffers, every part suffers with it; if one part is honored, every part rejoices with it."

As with Mildred and others who have suffered, we try to shoulder each other's burdens. We also rejoice with those who have reason to rejoice. The reasons for joy are varied: a long-infertile daughter learns she is expecting. A sister who once lingered in a coma is now sitting up in bed, answering her own telephone. A biopsy reads negative. A couple whose faith was dangling by a thread has reconnected to the Lord.

Oddly enough, I believe we do a better job of sharing suffering than rejoicing. We smile when we should laugh out loud. We clap politely when we should jump with joy. We pat each other on the back when we should be linked in a hearty embrace.

Picture the last time you were immersed in whole-hearted celebration. I remember years ago, watching the Abilene Christian University men's basketball team win game after game on their home court in ACU's Moody Coliseum. On the night the men broke the school's winning streak record, the building was rocking with chants and cheers. We had abandoned our seats much earlier in the game, and as the last shot was taken, the crowd erupted in loud whistles and whoops.

I was not a member of the basketball team. I was not dating a member of the team. In fact, I personally knew only one player. But I was a member of the student body. I was part of the school, and so were they. This was my team. We were their home crowd.

Every person gathered in the coliseum that night had a singular vision: our guys in purple and white shooting the hoops and breaking the records. We wanted this victory for the players, the school, and for ourselves. I have no doubt that the young men on the team were thrilled with the crowd's support and enthusiasm. The louder we yelled, the harder they played.

Imagine if our churches were filled with this kind of unified support and celebration. The

Breakfast Ministry Team cheers for the Vacation Bible School Team who chants for the Maintenance Crew who salutes the Drama Group who supports the Reception Committee who encourages the Ladies' Bible Class who endorse the Singles Ministry. When the Visitation Committee, or any other ministry, touches a life in the name of Christ, the crowd goes wild!

Gladness of heart — yours and mine — makes this scenario possible. And this is how:

First, we recognize our place in the body and our divine connection with our brothers and sisters.

Second, we commit ourselves to the leadership of the head, Christ.

Third, we key in on 1 Corinthians 12:26 and start rejoicing.

This decision, to get on with the business of rejoicing, may require great change. Perhaps we have been gladness-zappers rather than gladness-growers. A gladness-zapper may measure the length of the sermon rather than the depth. She may pay more attention to the attire of those serving the communion than the death that gave communion meaning. He may focus more on the unfamiliarity of the melody than the unchangeable Christ depicted in the song. She may fault the Benevolence Committee for consuming the budget rather than faithfully pray for those the committee has helped.

A gladness-grower takes the gladness of Christ and sends it coursing through the veins of the body, encouraging each body part to grow and thrive under the direction of the head. He seasons his speech with gentleness. She never exits the church without dispensing at least one positive comment to the servants who led the morning worship. He says, "How can I help?" rather than

"That's not my area." When gladness-growers hear good news, they spring into action.

The Vacation Bible School attracts more visitors than ever before, so the gladness-grower sends a card of thanks to the VBS coordinator, thanking her for her hours of service.

A teen-ager in the youth group lands the lead part in the school play, and a gladness-grower goes and sees the play.

A sister prays for healing, and she is healed. A gladness-grower makes immediate contact with the sister touched by God, and together they revel in the amazement of the moment.

A brother finds employment after months of stagnancy. A gladness-grower mails him a card of congratulations.

A church service goes overtime because there are several prayer requests. A gladness-grower shrugs off his previous plan for the afternoon and ministers to those who made the requests.

When budgets are being balanced, songs are being selected, potlucks are being planned, and curriculum is being created, the gladness-grower keeps one question in the forefront of his mind: How can we best further the kingdom of Christ? Perhaps he turns to Matthew 6:33: "Seek first his kingdom and his righteousness, and all these things will be given to you as well."

When the kingdom of Christ is furthered, the gladness-grower celebrates. What happened the last time someone was led to the baptistery in your church?

I love the way my husband concludes a baptism. When he pulls a dripping body up from the baptismal waters, he does two things. First, he hugs the new babe in Christ. Then he turns to the audience and says, "There's a party going on in heaven."

When a soul is saved, gladness-growers can't keep quiet. They praise God. They embrace the saved. They embrace the parents and other loved ones of the new Christian. They call friends and rejoice over the new life in Christ. Perhaps they plan a dinner party in honor of the new believer. Maybe they send flowers. Perhaps they mark the spiritual birthday in their calendars and send the sister in Christ flowers on her first spiritual anniversary.

People of gladness rejoice when others rejoice. They suffer when others suffer. Gladness-growers thank God for placing them in his body. They receive gladness from the body in times of trial, and give gladness to the body at every opportunity. And when a precious soul is saved, the gladness-growers throw a party.

# Study Guide

1.  Read 1 Corinthians 12:18 and explain the role you play within the body of Christ.

2.  Has your church body been a source of gladness in your life? If so, give at least two specific examples.
    1.
    2.

3.  a. Name three other ministries of your church body.
    1.
    2.
    3.

    b. Think of one way in which you can serve as a source of gladness to each of these.

4.  Envision the following scenario: A group of church members meets to plan a banquet honoring current and past elders. Different ideas are discussed, but participants cannot seem to agree on pertinent details. How would a gladness-zapper respond? How would a gladness-grower respond?

5.  Read 1 Corinthians 12:1-26. Remember the last person that was added to your church body. Pause and pray for this new Christian, asking God to guide you to be a source of gladness in the life of this new Christian.

# Gladness, Step-by-Step

I.   Seldom reflect on the changeless past.
   A. Realize that one heart cannot house both gladness and gloom.
   B. Use the Spirit's strength to cleanse your heart and head of sin and bitterness, so you can forgive, making room for the Spirit's gift of peace, goodness, and gladness.
   C. Savor the benefits of "seldom reflecting."

II.  Acknowledge God as alive, active, and working to occupy you.
   A. Regard every good and perfect gift as God's bid for your gladness, from the beauty of a starlit night to the success of a lifesaving operation.
   B. Remember God's efforts are not limited to the here and now. His occupation of you began in the beginning, continued with the sacrifice of his Son, and will persist for all eternity.

III. Embrace the occupation of God.
   A. Respond with the intensity of a child eager to open a pile of packages.
   B. Invite God to take control of your life, while you assume passenger status.
   C. Commit to obey God's love-based decrees.

IV. Get to know the giver of all gifts.
   A. Find a reading partner.
   B. Creatively saturate your surroundings with God.
   C. Re-energize your prayer life.

V. Meet every challenge with the heaven-or-earth litmus test.
   A. Keep your true source of gladness in the forefront of your mind as you experience temporary earthly circumstances.
   B. When faced with a major or minor challenge, determine if the situation is of an earthly or heavenly nature.

VI. Cultivate gladness, which will overflow into thanks.
   A. Recognize your blessings in a daily blessings book.
   B. Use a blessing to the benefit of someone else.

VII. Fortify and protect your newfound gladness.
   A. When gladness has escaped you, go to God.
   B. Work on your spiritual weaknesses before Satan does.
   C. Intentionally launch your own spiritual battles by means of active good works.

VIII. Allow God to carry you through pain.
   A. Realize nothing can separate you from the love of God.
   B. Remember that sadness does not displace gladness rooted in God.

IX. **Recognize your place in the body.**
   A. **Rejoice in the gladness to be gleaned from the body of Christ.**
   B. **Be a gladness-grower, not a gladness-zapper.**

"He seldom reflects
on the days of his life,
because God keeps him
occupied with
gladness of heart."

—Ecclesiastes 5:20

# Conclusion: Shout Out the Source!

"As I write this concluding chapter, I..."

I wrote the above seven words on August 6, 1997. I remember shutting down the computer and telling Lane that I had finally reached my conclusion and I wanted to pray about the last chapter.

My goal was to finish the book before the baby came, and I had about one week to go. But God had something else in mind. I gave birth to my second son, Jake, the very next day, August 7, at 1:09 p.m.

A mere sixteen days have passed since I wrote those first seven words. However, in that short window of time God has blessed me with experiences that have further cemented my faith in his timing and his occupation. In these same few weeks, God has also humbled me.

I now believe God wanted me to conclude this book on his timetable, not mine, because he had something to ask me: Are you willing to acknowledge my gladness, my timing, and my occupation to the world around you?

I developed complications with this pregnancy, as I did with Luke's. I was placed on bed rest until my induction date, slated for August 12. In the meantime, I was scheduled for regular blood pressure checks. I tried to change my August 7 checkup because Lane had the next day off and could watch our son while I visited the doctor. However, when I called, the nurse said I could not delay the check up even twenty-four hours. She wanted me in the next morning.

I agreed to come and asked a friend to stay with Luke. As the nurse checked my blood pressure, she remained silent. She left the room and came back with the doctor, who checked the pressure again and again. He told me we had reached a crisis, that we were "just waiting for a convulsion," and he scheduled a caesarean section for two hours later.

What if the nurse had said I could wait one more day?

What if I decided on my own I simply had to wait and refused to keep the appointment?

What if I couldn't find Lane?

What if I couldn't find anyone to stay with Luke?

What if I did convulse before reaching the hospital?

What if? What if? God, in his occupation, took care of each "what if." Everything fell into place. Lane was reachable and able to be home within minutes to take me to the hospital. My friend, Amanda, was able to stay with Luke until family arrived. My mom, who lives eight hours away, was able to fly in immediately. Although the hospital admitting area was packed, I was able to check in and was taken to the operating room fifteen minutes ahead of schedule. While my blood pressure remained high during the surgery, as soon as Jake was born, I was fine. And Jake weighed in at a healthy six pounds, fifteen ounces. Blessing after blessing after blessing, crammed into one morning and early afternoon.

I had absolutely no problem sharing this evidence of God's timing with other Christians in my family and my Christian friends. However, as I discovered one week later, I did not feel at ease explaining this to my neighbors.

The family who lives next door came over to bring Jake a gift. Mrs. Bailey asked me the details of our experience, and I elaborated on how perfectly every thing worked out. She expressed her amazement. As the conversation continued, I wanted to say, "It was God," but I did not know if the time was right. Would she understand? What would she think of me? I mean, we had invited these neighbors to church once before, and they knew Lane was a minister, but still…

Eventually, I said, "I know it was divine intervention." The words sounded stiff and awkward, and I cringed in embarrassment before God. I shook myself, came to my spiritual senses, and finally said, "It was God."

I was glad, so very glad, at the safe arrival of my son, but I could not tell a neighbor the core reason for my gladness without stammering and stuttering. When I finally told her, "God," she nodded and smiled her acknowledgment. Not only had I sold God short, I sold her short as well. She understood perfectly.

Shout out the source!

I hope and pray I never again hesitate in naming my gladness source to everyone, whether or not I know their spiritual interest. I especially want to share my gladness with those who do not know Jesus. What better way to draw others to God than to boldly echo the words of Psalm 66:5: "Come and see what God has done, how awesome his works in man's behalf!"

As we've mentioned, growing gladness of heart encompasses a bounty of personal benefits. We accept a God who infiltrates our hearts with his Spirit. This Spirit is our endless source of strength, patience, forgiveness, and countless other emotions and godly attributes. We discover our saved condition, made possible by the sacrifice of the Son of God. Rather than reflecting on past pain, we revel in the love of God and his forgiveness of us. We actively seek to know him and acknowledge daily the blessings he pours into our lives. When our hearts ache, he carries and cradles us.

As we respond to God's occupation of our lives, we grow gladness of heart, which manifests itself in our thoughts, our words, our expressions, and our attitudes. Our joy is not characterized by giddy giggles, but a warm heart rooted in the knowledge of the love of God. We begin to think, feel, and act differently. Days are brighter as earthly cares are placed in proper perspective. Relationships are sweeter as we incorporate the word of God into our actions and reactions with others. We exude peace and joy as we place our lives in the hands of the Creator of the universe.

I could write on and on about the fruits of the gladness of God—what we have received and how much better our lives have become. However, in reveling in our blessings, we should not grow self-centered, focusing only on what God has done for us. As we read the Bible in its entirety, we will find that along with gladness comes responsibility.

When God gave you his Son, his Spirit, and his gladness, he did two things: He made you a new person, and he gave you a ministry.

Therefore, if anyone is in Christ, he is a new creation; the old has gone, the new has come! All this is from God, who reconciled himself to us through Christ and gave us the ministry of reconciliation… We are therefore Christ's ambassadors, as though God were making his appeal through us. (2 Corinthians 5:17-18,20).

God made us into new people through Jesus Christ. We, in turn, are given the responsibility of letting God work in us to introduce others to Jesus Christ — our ministry of reconciliation.

Countless books have been written and lessons taught on our responsibility of evangelism. To delve into the topic would require writing another book. However, we cannot close our study on gladness without linking it to our God-given ministry.

We can and should use our newfound gladness of heart to entice the world around us to the Gladness-Giver. When you experience a gift from God, tell someone. Don't just tell them what the gift was; tell them about the Gift-Giver. When someone asks you about your gentleness of spirit or your willingness to forgive another, tell them Who is responsible for your actions.

Be intentional in your efforts to share your gladness. And be ready. Paul tells the believers in Colosse:

Be wise in the way you act toward outsiders; make the most of every opportunity. Let your conversation be always full of grace, seasoned with salt, so that you may know how to answer everyone (Colossians 4:5-6).

Let's introduce others to God by seasoning our conversation with his name. We do not have to make our task more difficult than God intended it to be. We do not have to speak in poetic verse, or memorize pages and pages of Bible text. We simply tell people: God.

Suppose we are in the front yard with neighbors and watching a beautiful sunset. We say, "God sure knows how to make a sunset, doesn't he?"

Our co-workers are talking about the successful surgery of an office mate, and we say, "God answered my prayer."

Someone comments on our calmness in the midst of a trying situation, so we say, "God gave me patience."

Our boss mentions the amount of time we spend at church. We say, "Here's what God has done for me…"

If anyone expresses the slightest interest in our new attitude, we should use the conversation as a springboard to tell him or her about God.

When you and I are moved to share the gladness of God with someone else, let's not allow Satan to restrain us. The God-inspired good news of our lives can introduce someone else to the Good News of Jesus Christ.

Let's not hoard our gladness. We'll cherish it. Grow in it. Revel in it. Take refuge in it. Heal in it. Rest in it. But most importantly: tell it.

> In that day, you will say, "Give thanks to the Lord, call on his name; make known among the nations what he has done, and proclaim that his name is exalted. Sing to the Lord, for he has done glorious things; let his be known to all the world" (Isaiah 12:4-5).

Shout out the source!

# *Gladness, Step-by-Step*

I.  Seldom reflect on the changeless past.
    A. Realize that one heart cannot house both gladness and gloom.
    B. Use the Spirit's strength to cleanse your heart and head of sin and bitterness, so you can forgive, making room for the Spirit's gift of peace, goodness, and gladness.
    C. Savor the benefits of "seldom reflecting."

II. Acknowledge God as alive, active, and working to occupy you.
    A. Regard every good and perfect gift as God's bid for your gladness, from the beauty of a starlit night to the success of a lifesaving operation.
    B. Remember God's efforts are not limited to the here and now. His occupation of you began in the beginning, continued with the sacrifice of his Son, and will persist for all eternity.

III. Embrace the occupation of God.
    A. Respond with the intensity of a child eager to open a pile of packages.
    B. Invite God to take control of your life, while you assume passenger status.
    C. Commit to obey God's love-based decrees.

IV. Get to know the giver of all gifts.
    A. Find a reading partner.
    B. Creatively saturate your surroundings with God.
    C. Re-energize your prayer life.

V. Meet every challenge with the heaven-or-earth litmus test.
   A. Keep your true source of gladness in the forefront of your mind as you experience temporary earthly circumstances.
   B. When faced with a major or minor challenge, determine if the situation is of an earthly or heavenly nature.

VI. Cultivate gladness, which will overflow into thanks.
   A. Recognize your blessings in a daily blessings book.
   B. Use a blessing to the benefit of someone else.

VII. Fortify and protect your newfound gladness.
   A. When gladness has escaped you, go to God.
   B. Work on your spiritual weaknesses before Satan does.
   C. Intentionally launch your own spiritual battles by means of active good works.

VIII. Allow God to carry you through pain.
   A. Realize nothing can separate you from the love of God.
   B. Remember that sadness does not displace gladness rooted in God.

IX. Recognize your place in the body.
   A. Rejoice in the gladness to be gleaned from the body of Christ.
   B. Be a gladness-grower, not a gladness-zapper.

X.  **Shout out the source.**
    A.  **Accept your God-given ministry of reconciliation.**
    B.  **Use your newfound gladness to bring others to God.**

*"He seldom reflects on the days of his life, because God keeps him occupied with gladness of heart."*

—Ecclesiastes 5:20